Rijal

Rijal

Narrators of the Muwaṭṭaʾ al-Imām Muḥammad

Shaykh ʿAbd al-Ḥayy al-Laknawī

Ta-Ha Publishers Ltd.
1 Wynne Road
London SW9 0BB

Published by:
Ta-Ha Publishers Ltd.
1 Wynne Road
London SW9 0BB

By: ᶜAbd al-Ḥayy al-Laknawī
General Editor: Afsar Siddiqui
Translated by: Abdaṣṣamad Clarke
Edited by: Shaykh Sulaymān Gani
Cover by: Abdaṣṣamad Clarke

British Library Cataloguing in Publication Data
al-Ḥayy, ᶜAbd
Rijāl
1. Muḥammad ibn al-Ḥasan ash-Shaybānī 2. Islamic law
Sources
1. Title
340.5 ' 9

ISBN 1 842000497

Typeset by: Bookwright.
Email: bookwright@bogvaerker.dk
Web-site: http://www.bogvaerker.dk/Bookwright
Printed by: Deluxe Printers, London. Tel: 0208-965 1771

Preface

This book is a compilation from entries in *at-Taʿlīq al-mumajjad* – Shaykh ʿAbd al-Ḥayy al-Laknawī's commentary on the *Muwaṭṭaʾ al-Imām Muḥammad* – which go into some detail on the narrators of the ḥadīth and traditions in that book, most particularly their standing as narrators.

Rijāl will be included in the translation of *Muwaṭṭaʾ al-Imām Muḥammad* to be published later in the year by Turāth Publishing, inshāʾAllāh. Nevertheless, the book is self-sufficient and will be of use to whoever would like a sense of how critical scholars evaluate these narrators, among whom are many of the great authorities of the Companions, the Followers, and Followers of the Followers.

The book is laid out alphabetically according to the English alphabet. Names beginning with *ʿayn* are thus included under A, I and U. In names beginning with the definite article *al*, we ignore that for the purposes of listing the name. Although we have followed transliteration conventions, there are some small matters on which we differ: first, we do not retain *al* in front of 'sun' letters but show them assimilated as for example in *ash-shams* rather than *al-shams*.

Contents

Introduction

The Narrators

Introduction

The Sunnah of the Prophet ﷺ – his noble ḥadīth, his sayings, doings, and affirmations – enjoyed the good fortune from the very beginning of complete meticulous care and being acted upon by the noble Companions and the outstanding Followers, so that it was completely safeguarded and transmitted in minute detail in realisation of the saying of Allah ﷻ:

> It is We Who have sent down the Reminder
> and We Who will preserve it.
> (Sūrat al-Ḥijr: 9)

A part of the preservation of the Reminder and the Noble Book is its preservation – the Sunnah's – because it explains it [the Book] and makes its judgements and its aims specific. He said ﷺ:

> And We have sent down the Reminder to you
> so that you can make clear to mankind
> what has been sent down to them
> (Sūrat an-Nahl: 44)

The situation of Madīnah in the Sunnah

Every city which Islam opened up and in which the Muslims became settled had its portion of knowledge which differed from each other sometimes a little but sometimes a great deal according to the number of the Companions who came to it and resided there. The portion of the Abode of the Prophetic Emigration – Madīnah al-Munawwarah – was the fullest portion because of the abundance of Companions there, since it, and Makkah al-Mukarramah after its opening to Islam, were the first Dār al-Islām and the place for which the Muslims' hearts longed.

The Sunnah lived in it, there it overflowed and spread in all the lands of Islam and it was inherited by people, generation from generation, tribe from tribe. The number of fuqahāʾ and ḥadīth scholars multiplied extensively, for it has been transmitted that Mālik said, "I showed this book of mine to seventy of the fuqahāʾ of Madīnah." When Mālik was growing up the Sunnah had taken the path towards being recorded and registered.

Madīnah's precedence in the recording of the Sunnah

The Sunnah was recorded in Madīnah al-Munawwarah before all of the other great capital cities. Imām Muḥammad ibn Shihāb az-Zuhrī (died 124 AH) the Madīnan and shaykh of Mālik composed in it, Mūsā ibn ʿUqbah (died 114 AH) the Madīnan and another shaykh of Mālik, Muḥammad ibn Isḥāq al-Muṭṭalibī (died 151 AH) the Madīnan, and Ibn Abī Dhiʾb Muḥammad ibn ʿAbd ar-Raḥmān (died 198 AH) the Madīnan.

During the lives of these men and after them other imāms of the ḥadīth and the Sunnah composed works in Makkah al-Mukarramah, Kūfa, Baṣra, and Khurāsān, but the first place in recording the Sunnah belongs to the notable people of knowledge of Madīnah al-Munawwarah

Imām Mālik's composition of the *Muwaṭṭaʾ*

Imām Mālik's composition of the *Muwaṭṭaʾ* comes among the number of books which record the Sunnah in Madīnah and elsewhere (the Ten Books) in terms of recording and is the first in terms of compiling it according to fiqh categories.

The people of knowledge mention that Imām Mālik's composition of the *Muwaṭṭaʾ* was only because of the suggestion of the Abbasid khalīfah Abū Jaʿfar al-Manṣūr made during one of his Ḥajj journeys. Al-Manṣūr invited him to visit him and Abū Jaᶜfar honoured him and made him sit beside him asking him many questions. His manner, knowledge, intellect, the penetration of his thinking and the soundness of his answers pleased him and he recognised his station in knowledge, in the dīn and as an imām of the Muslims.

The noted scholar and historian Qāḍī Imām Ibn Khaldūn said in his *Muqaddimah*:

> Abū Jaᶜfar had a rank in knowledge and in the dīn before the khilāfah and after it. It was he who said to Mālik while indicating to him to compose the *Muwaṭṭa*ʾ, "Abū ᶜAbdullāh, no one remains on the face of the earth more knowledgeable than me or you, but the khilāfah has occupied me. You must compose a book for people by which they will benefit. In it you should avoid the concessions (*rukhṣah*) that Ibn ᶜAbbās grants, the severities of Ibn ᶜUmar, and the unusual and singular positions (*shādhdh*) that Ibn Masᶜūd takes. Arrange it and make it accessible (*waṭṭi*ʾ)[1] for people." Mālik said, "By Allah! He taught me composition on that day."

Imām Mālik composed the *Muwaṭṭa*ʾ according to the method which Abū Jaᶜfar al-Manṣūr had indicated. He compiled the choicest of the ḥadīth and the traditions narrated among the People of Madīnah, and he gathered the practice (*ᶜamal*) which was transmitted by large numbers of one generation to large numbers of the next generation (*tawātur*), avoiding the concessions granted by Ibn ᶜAbbās, the severities of Ibn ᶜUmar and the singular and unusual positions adopted by Ibn Masᶜūd, confining himself in narrating only from the shaykhs of the People of Madīnah except for six people: Abū'z-Zubayr from Makkah, Ibrāhīm ibn Abī ᶜAblah from Shām, ᶜAbd al-Karīm ibn Mālik from al-Jazīrah (north-west ᶜIrāq), ᶜAṭāʾ ibn ᶜAbdullāh from Khurāsān, Ḥumayd aṭ-Ṭawīl and Ayyūb as-Sakhtiyānī from Baṣra. He completed the work in the khilāfah of al-Mahdī.

[1] His command *waṭṭi*ʾ comprises the senses of facilitating, making something easy, accessible and smoothing a path, and it is from this that one meaning of the name *Muwaṭṭa*ʾ derives: The Smoothed and Levelled Path Made Easy for People.

Thus was completed the composition of this book the *Muwaṭṭa'* in which Imām Mālik collected the ḥadīth of the Messenger of Allah ﷺ and the verdicts of the Companions and the Followers, and the view which he considered the consensus of the People of Madīnah which he did not leave. So he collected together the ḥadīth in the widest sense and whatever is connected to them of the traditions of the first generation because they are the major reference for practical rulings.

The number of ḥadīth and traditions narrated in the *Muwaṭṭa'*

Al-Abhurī Abū Bakr said, "The sum total of what is in the *Muwaṭṭa'* of traditions from the Prophet ﷺ, and from the Companions and the Followers is one thousand, seven hundred and twenty ḥadīth, of which those with a chain of transmission are six hundred, the mursal ḥadīth [ascribed directly to the Prophet ﷺ without mentioning the Companion or Companions from whom it was heard] two hundred and twenty-two, and the mawqūf [statements made without ascribing them to the Prophet ﷺ] six hundred and thirteen. Of the verdicts of the Followers there are two hundred and eighty-five."

The particular merits of the *Muwaṭṭa'*

The *Muwaṭṭa'* has very many particular merits by which it is distinguished from the other books of ḥadīth which I shall mention here briefly:

First, that it is the composion of an imām who was a faqīh and a scholar of ḥadīth, a major mujtahid (person who could exert his intellect to arrive at a judgement) whose judgement is followed, about whose imāmate in fiqh and in ḥadīth the imāms of his own age and subsequent ages testifed without there being any dispute.

Second, the Imām of the Imāms, faqīh, ḥadīth scholar and mujtahid Imām ash-Shāfiʿī bore witness to the *Muwaṭṭaʾ*, and he is sufficient for you. He said:

> There is not on the surface of the earth a book which is more ṣaḥīḥ after the Book of Allah than the book of Mālik

Third, that it is one of the compositions from the middle of the second century of the hijrah, so that it precedes everything and is preceded by nothing else since it is the first book in its category, and whatever precedes has superiority. He was the Imām who laid the path for composition of works on ḥadīth according to the categories of fiqh and all the trustworthy ones after him modelled themselves on him such as ʿAbdullāh ibn al-Mubārak, al-Bukhārī, Muslim, Saʿīd ibn Manṣūr, Abū Dāwūd, at-Tirmidhī, an-Nasāʾī, Ibn Mājah and others.

A brief biographical notice on Imām Mālik the author of the Muwaṭṭaʾ

He was Mālik ibn Anas ibn Mālik al-Aṣbaḥī al-Ḥimyarī the Madīnan, Abū ʿAbdullāh, the Imām of the Abode of the Hijrah, one of the four Imāms. He was born and died in Madīnah. He was firm in his dīn, remote from the rulers and kings. He was denounced to Jaʿfar the uncle of al-Manṣūr al-ʿAbbāsī who had him flogged which dislocated his shoulder. Ar-Rashīd sent for him to come to him and narrate ḥadīth to him and he said, "Amīr al-Muʾminīn, knowledge is come to, it does not come. It is visited, it does not visit." So ar-Rashīd went to his house and leaned against the wall.[2] Mālik said, "Amīr al-Muʾminīn, a part of honouring the Messenger of Allah ﷺ is honouring knowledge," and so he went and sat before him.

His prestige covered the horizons, so that the people of the cities and the provinces narrated ḥadīth in his name, and his fatwās were widely published and called to mind in Egypt, Shām and all the lands of the west. In

[2] In some accounts, ar-Rashīd sat down on a small raised seat on which Imām Mālik ordinarily sat in order to teach.

Andalus he was the Imām along with whom no other imām was mentioned. He had authority in Madīnah which reached to the degree of the authorities who governed it.

Allah chose Mālik with a quality which clung to him, i.e. awe. The rulers were in awe of him, and they would feel humbled in his presence. The awe they had of him reached a limit such as kings and amirs did not attain, so he was held in awe even though he had no authority.

Mālik lived highly esteemed in himself, and honoured by people until he died in 179 AH.

The *Muwaṭṭa'* of Imām Muḥammad

Ḥāfiẓ Muḥammad ibn ᶜAbdullāh ad-Dimashqī, better known as Ibn Nāṣir ad-Dīn, made the number of narrators of the *Muwaṭṭa'* reach to eighty-three narrators, the most famous of which in this age among the people of the east is that of Muḥammad ibn al-Ḥasan ash-Shaybānī and among the people of the west that of Yaḥyā al-Laythī.

The former is distinguished by its explanations of that which the people of ᶜIrāq adhered to of the recorded ḥadīth of the Ḥijāz in the *Muwaṭṭa'*. and that which they did not adhere to because of other proofs which Muḥammad derives in his *Muwaṭṭa'*. It is very useful for those who wish to compare the views of the people of Madīnah and of the people of ᶜIrāq and it explains the proofs of the two groups.

The latter is distinguished along with the other narrations of the *Muwaṭṭa'* apart from Imām Muḥammad's in that it contains the record of the *ᶜamal* – the practice of the People of Madīnah – and the explanations of Mālik, comprising something like three thousand cases in categories of fiqh.[3]

One of the merits of the the *Muwaṭṭa'* of Imām Muḥammad is that its narrator – Imām Muḥammad ibn al-Ḥasan ash-Shaybānī – is a faqīh, a

[3] See *The Origins of Islamic Law* by Yasin Dutton, pp 22-26.

major ḥadīth scholar and someone who is followed in his own right, to whose imāmate in fiqh, ḥadīth and Arabic language others have born witness. He stayed close to his shaykh Mālik for three years, and heard the book from him in his own words so he filled up and was quenched, he drank, and he drank in large draughts from his understanding, knowledge and narration, along with what he had of unusual penetration of intellect, complete intelligence, and possession of the faculty of discernment in himself.

Another merit of it is that Imām Muḥammad ibn al-Ḥasan ash-Shaybānī was the pupil of the two Imāms, Imām Abū Ḥanīfah and Abū Yūsuf, he was the shaykh of Imām ash-Shāfiʿī, and he skilfully narrated from his own shaykh Mālik. After narrating the ḥadīth of a chapter he added in an explanation of his madhhab on the issue, whether in agreement or in disagreement, and an explanation of the madhhab of his shaykh Imām Abū Ḥanīfah, and his agreement or disagreement, and sometimes an explanation of the madhhab of his shaykh Imām Mālik, and also the madhhab of people in general of our fuqahāʾ. Because of the great number of ḥadīth which he narrates in it from people other than Mālik, and because of the great amount of his own exertions of intellect to reach a judgement and his own fiqh which he includes in it, and the fiqh of Imām Abū Ḥanīfah and others, almost in every single chapter, and the madhhabs of some of the Companions in some of the chapters, then this book became famous as the *Muwaṭṭaʾ Imām Muḥammad.*

It is not strange that the *Muwaṭṭaʾ* of Muḥammad is not simply a book which he narrated literally as the narrator had heard it from the author without adding anything extra or making any commentary on it or corrections. On the contrary, it is a book in which is the fiqh of Imām Muḥammad, the fiqh of his shaykh Imām Abū Ḥanīfah and the fiqh of our Ḥanafī people in general who preceded Imām Muḥammad, and the madhhabs of some of the Companions, also some discussion of the positions that Mālik and others took.

It is a record of the fiqh of the people of ḥadīth, of exertion of the intellect to arrive at a judgement (*ijtihād*) and of theoretical understanding (*ra᾽y*) of the Ḥijāz and ʿIrāq along with a comparison of these madhhabs and theoretical understandings as they apply to cases. This is an extremely precious extra merit for whoever grasps and recognises its value. So it is not strange that the *Muwaṭṭa᾽* should be ascribed to Imām Muḥammad because it is narrated from him and because he added many ḥadīth into and added a great deal of knowledge into it connected to the fiqh of ḥadīth, and the rulings of each chapter and the comparison of different exertions of the intellect to arrive at judgements.

As for the number of ḥadīth ascribed directly to the Prophet ﷺ and traditions which stop short at Companions and those who came after them which are in the *Muwaṭṭa᾽* of Imām Muḥammad, whether with or without chains of transmission, they are in total one thousand, one hundred and eighty, of which those which are transmitted by way of Mālik are one thousand and five, and those which are transmitted through others are one hundred and seventy-five, and those which are transmitted from Abū Ḥanīfah are thirteen, those from Abū Yūsuf are four, and the rest are from other people.

A small fragment in biographical notice on Imām Muḥammad the narrator of the *Muwaṭṭa᾽*

He was Muḥammad ibn al-Ḥasan ibn Farqad ash-Shaybānī, one of the mawlās of [the tribe of] Shayban. He was Abū ʿAbdullāh, an imām in fiqh and in the science of the principles of fiqh. It was he who spread the knowledge of Imām Abū Ḥanīfah. He was originally from the village of Ḥarsatā in al-Ghūṭah – the fertile oasis to the south of Damascus. He was born in Wāsiṭ in 131 AH and grew up in Kūfa. He listened to Imām Abū Ḥanīfah whose madhhab became dominant in his thinking and for which he was known. Then he moved to Baghdād and ar-Rashīd appointed him qāḍī of ar-Riqqah.

Ash-Shāfiʿī said, "If I wished to say that the Qurʾān was revealed in the language of Muḥammad ibn al-Ḥasan, I would say so, because of the purity of his language."

Ḥāfiẓ adh-Dhahabī said, "He succeeded to the leadership in fiqh in ʿIrāq after Abū Yūsuf, and imāms learnt their fiqh from him. He compiled compilations, and he was one of the sharpest intellects in the world. He was appointed chief Qāḍī by ar-Rashīd and he attained unsurpassed rank, prestige and entourage. Ash-Shāfiʿī considered him a definitive proof in ḥadīth, and it is related of him that he had sharp incisive thinking in superabundance, complete intellect, pre-eminent authority and a great deal of recitation."

So this is a small glimmer from the biographical notice of Imām Muḥammad ibn al-Ḥasan who narrated the *Muwaṭṭaʾ* from Imām Mālik and may He reward them both on behalf of knowledge, the dīn and of the Muslims with the best reward.

At-Taʿlīq al-mumajjad – the commentary on the *Muwaṭṭaʾ* of Imām Muḥammad

A large group of the earlier and later scholars have written commentaries on the *Muwaṭṭaʾ* of Yaḥyā, but only three scholars have written commentaries on the *Muwaṭṭaʾ* of Imām Muḥammad: Bīrizādah, ʿAlī al-Qārī and Shaykh ʿAbd al-Ḥayy al-Laknawī.

There is no doubt that the book *at-Taʿlīq al-mumajjad ʿalā Muwaṭṭaʾ Muḥammad* is a tremendous book and a magnificent commentary from Imām ʿAbd al-Ḥayy al-Laknawī. He began its composition towards the end of 1292 AH at the age of twenty-seven years old, but he was interrupted by travels, various accidental happenings and things that occupied him, so that he completed his composition in Shaʿbān 1295.

It is an astonishing talent and a remarkable ability that a young man who was Indian both in abode and linguistically should scale the heights of the *Muwaṭṭa᾽* at the age which he did. He included in it the most splendid and radiant of his knowledge and the highest of his cognisance of the noble ḥadīth and its sciences, Ḥanafī fiqh, the other madhhabs and every other science which even in the least way is connected to it. This book came like a matchless pearl and one of the most precious jewels of knowledge.

The reader who studies it will find merits within it by which Imām al-Laknawī is distinguished and will be astonished at the strength of his talent and his mastery of precise and accurate determination, accuracy and thoroughness, his discussion of the relative positions of the madhhabs and different views, distinguishing which of them are weightier or weaker, his independence, impartiality and fairness without twising the texts and without being directionless.

Similarly the reader will find him mentioning the biographical notices of the narrators who occur in the chains of transmission, their states and what is connected to regarding them as trustworthy or weak narrators, but without any partisan spirit because of madhhab affiliation, so that the condition of the ḥadīth becomes completely clear in terms of its soundness or weakness.

Mawlānā Niᶜmatullāh al-Azami

Teacher of ḥadīth, Dar al-Ulum, Deoband, India

الرِّجَالُ

The Narrators

A

"A man" [ḥadīth 821]. There is in the *Muwaṭṭa*ᵓ of Yaḥyā and its commentary, "Mālik from Muḥammad ibn ᶜAbdullāh ibn Abī Maryam al-Khuzāᶜī." Abū Ḥātim said, "A right-acting Madīnan shaykh," and Ibn Ḥibbān mentioned him in *ath-Thiqāt* that he was the one who asked Saᶜīd ibn al-Musayyab, and so by that the unknown man is made known.

"A narrator who is trustworthy to me" [ḥadīth 716]. Az-Zurqānī said, "Some say that it was Makhramah ibn Bukayr or Ibn Luhayᶜah, because al-Walīd ibn Muslim narrated it from ᶜAbdullāh ibn Luhayᶜah."

Abān ibn ᶜUthmān ibn ᶜAffān – [son of] the Amīr al-Muᵓminīn and of the third of the Khulafāᵓ who took the right way – Abū ᶜAbdullāh the Madīnan was a Follower who had many narrations and who was a trustworthy narrator. He died in 105 AH.

ᶜAbbād ibn al-ᶜAwwām. Adh-Dhahabī said in *Tadhkirat al-ḥuffāẓ*, "ᶜAbbād ibn al-ᶜAwwām the imām and scholar of ḥadīth Abū Sahl al-Wāsiṭī. Abū Dāwūd and others regarded him as a trustworthy narrator. Ibn Saᶜd said, 'He was one of the noble men in every respect.' He had become a shīᶜah and ar-Rashīd imprisoned him for a time and then later released him, and so he resided in Baghdād. There is disagreement about the date of his death after 180 AH and some say three, five, six and seven years after that. There is agreement about using him as a decisive proof." (Abridged)

ᶜAbbād ibn Tamīm ibn Ghaziyyah al-Māzinī. He narrated from his father – and he was a Companion – and from his paternal uncle ᶜAbdullāh ibn Zayd al-Māzinī. An-Nasāʾī and others declared him a trustworthy narrator, as as-Suyūṭī said.

ᶜAbbād ibn Ziyād was a mawlā of al-Mughīrah ibn Shuᶜbah and not one of his children as narrated.

ᶜAbd al-ᶜAzīz ibn Ḥakīm. Ibn Ḥibbān mentioned him among the trustworthy narrators of the Followers, where he said, "ᶜAbd al-ᶜAzīz ibn Ḥakīm al-Ḥaḍramī whose kunyā was Abū Yaḥyā. He narrated from Ibn ᶜUmar and is counted among the people of Kūfa. From him narrated ath-Thawrī and Isrāʾīl. He died after 130 AH. He is the one who is usually called Ibn Abī Ḥakīm." In *Mīzān al-iᶜtidāl* there is that Ibn Maᶜīn said he was a trustworthy narrator, but that Abū Ḥātim said, "He is not strong."

ᶜAbd al-Jabbār [ḥadīth 647]. ᶜAbd al-Jabbār ibn ᶜAbbās al-Hamdānī [rather than ᶜAbd al-Jabbār *from* Ibn ᶜAbbās al-Hamdānī, in the view of ᶜAbd al-Ḥayy al-Laknawī]. He said in *Tahdhīb at-tahdhīb*, "ᶜAbd al-Jabbār ibn al-ᶜAbbās ash-Shibāmī al-Hamdānī the Kūfan. Shibām is a mountain in the Yemen. He narrated from Abū Isḥāq as-Sabīᶜī, ᶜAdī ibn Thābit, Salamah ibn Kuhayl, Qays ibn Wahb, ᶜAwn, ᶜUthmān ibn al-Mughīrah ath-Thaqafī, ᶜUrayb ibn Marthad al-Mashriqī and a number of others, and from him narrated Ibn al-Mubārak, Ismāᶜīl ibn Muḥammad ibn Juḥādah, Muslim ibn Qutaybah, Ibrāhīm ibn Yūsuf ibn Abī Isḥāq as-Sabīᶜī, Abū Aḥmad az-Zubayrī, al-Ḥasan ibn Ṣāliḥ, Wakīᶜ and others. ᶜAbdullāh ibn Aḥmad [ibn Ḥanbal] said from his father, 'I hope that there is no harm in him, and he used to be a Shīᶜah.' Ibn Maᶜīn and Abū Dāwūd said, 'There is no harm in him.' Abū Ḥātim said he was a trustworthy narrator. Al-Bazzār said, 'His ḥadīth are straight.' Al-ᶜIjlī said, 'A little right-acting person (*ṣuwayliḥ*) in whom there is no harm.'" (Abridged) There is in *Ansāb as-Samᶜānī* after mention that ash-Shibāmī derives from Shibām a land in the Yemen, "The person who is well known with respect to it is ᶜAbd al-Jabbār ibn ᶜAbbās ash-Shibāmī al-Hamdānī one of the people of Kūfa. Ḥe narrated from ᶜAwn ibn Abī Juḥayfah and ᶜAṭāʾ ibn as-Sāʾib, and from him narrated Ibn Abī Zāʾidah and the Kūfans. He was in the main a Shīᶜah."

ᶜAbd al-Karīm ibn Abi'l-Mukhāriq. Two [narrators] are called ᶜAbd al-Karīm, the first of whom is a trustworthy narrator about whom there is agreement, and from whom al-Bukhārī and Muslim narrated, and he is Ibn Mālik al-Jazarī and his kunyā was Abū Saᶜd. The second was Ibn Abi'l-Mukhāriq whose kunyā was Abū Umayyah, and he is to be abandoned, as is in *al-Qawl al-musaddad fi'dh-dhibb ᶜan musnad Aḥmad* by Ḥāfiẓ Ibn Ḥajar al-ᶜAsqalānī. He said in *at-Tamhīd,* "He is weak, about which the people of ḥadīth are unanimous. He was a teacher in a Qurʾān school, of a good way of life, and his way of living deceived Mālik [about his qualities as a narrator of ḥadīth], for he was not one of the people of his town so that he could know him. He died in 126 AH or 127 AH. As-Suyūṭī said in *Mirqāt aṣ-ṣuᶜūd,* 'It is not sound in that which ᶜAbd al-Karīm ibn Abi'l-Mukhāriq alone narrates to judge that he fabricated, because Mālik narrated from him, and it is well known that it was his habit only to narrate from those he regarded as trustworthy narrators even if others discovered what necessarily required taking a critical view of him.'" The name of Ibn Abi'l-Mukhāriq is said to have been Qays but some say Ṭāriq.

ᶜAbd al-Karīm al-Jazarī was ᶜAbd al-Karīm ibn Mālik al-Jazarī Abū Saᶜīd al-Ḥarrānī and he was one of those who were firmly established and one whom the imāms regarded as a trustworthy narrator. Ibn Maᶜīn said that he was a firmly established trustworthy narrator. Ibn Saᶜd said, "He was a trustworthy narrator who had many ḥadīth." He died in 127 AH. He is not the same as ᶜAbd al-Karīm ibn Abi'l-Mukhāriq Abū

Umayyah the Baṣran about whom there is disagreement, but they are often confused for each other, as is in *Muqaddimah Fatḥ al-bārī* by Ḥāfiẓ ibn Ḥajar and others. Al-Jazarī is by ascription to the Jazīrah (island or peninsula) of Ibn ʿUmar which was a place built up and populated by a man well known as Ibn ʿUmar who is not ʿAbdullāh ibn ʿUmar the Companion. Ibn al-Athīr al-Jazarī, the author of *an-Nihāyah fī gharīb al-ḥadīth* and *Jāmiʿ al-uṣūl,* is also ascribed to him. As-Suyūṭī said in *Lubb al-lubāb fī taḥrīr al-ansāb,* "Al-Jazarī is by ascription to a number of lands: Mawṣil, Sanjār, Ḥarrān, ar-Rahā, ar-Riqqah, Ra'sʿAyn, Āmid, Diyārbakr and the island of Ibn ʿUmar." In the *Jāmiʿ al-uṣūl,* "It is by ascription to the island, which is the land between the Euphrates and the Tigris among which are Diyārbakr and Rabīʿah."

ʿAbd al-Majīd ibn Suhayl and az-Zuhrī [ḥadīth 820]. This is how it is found in many copies of this book, and similarly in a copy upon which is the commentary of al-Qārī. Apparently it shows that Mālik had two shaykhs for this narration who both narrated from Ibn al-Musayyab, first, ʿAbd al-Majīd, and second, az-Zuhrī. However, it seems that the "and" which precedes az-Zuhrī is a mistake of the copyist and that really it is a descriptive name for ʿAbd al-Majīd himself [that he was from Banī Zuhrah], and that he alone is the shaykh of Mālik in this narration. There is disagreement about his name, and some say ʿAbd al-Majīd as in this book, and some say ʿAbd al-Ḥamīd which is incorrect. In the *Muwaṭṭa'* of Yaḥyā and its commentary by az-Zurqānī there is, "'Mālik from ʿAbd al-Ḥamīd,' which is how Yaḥyā, Ibn Nāfiʿ and Ibn Yūsuf narrated it. The dominant majority of the narrators of the *Muwaṭṭa'* say ʿAbd al-Majīd, and it is the one which is well known, and this is how al-Bukhārī and al-ʿUqaylī mention it, and it is the correct position and the truth about which there is no doubt. The former [ʿAbd al-Ḥamīd] is a mistake, as Abū ʿUmar [Ibn ʿAbd al-Barr] said, "Ibn Suhayl is the husband of Thurayyā bint ʿAbdullāh ibn ʿAbd ar-Raḥmān ibn ʿAwf az-Zuhrī and he is a trustworthy narrator who may be adduced as a proof. He has only this single marfūc ḥadīth in the *Muwaṭṭa*ʾ narrated from Ibn al-Musayyab." In *Iscāf al-mubaṭṭa*ʾ of as-Suyūṭī, "cAbd al-Majīd ibn Suhayl ibn cAbd ar-Raḥmān ibn cAwf az-Zuhrī Abū Muḥammad the Madīnan who narrated from his paternal uncle Abū Salamah, Sacīd ibn al-Musayyab, and Abū Ṣāliḥ Dhakwān, and from whom Mālik, ad-Darāwardī and others narrated. An-Nasāʾī and Ibn Macīn declared him to be a trustworthy narrator." There is the like of that in *at-Taqrīb*, *al-Kāshif* and elsewhere.

cAbd al-Mālik ibn Abī Bakr is cAbd al-Mālik ibn Abī Bakr ibn cAbd ar-Raḥmān ibn al-Ḥārith ibn Hishām of Makhzūm, the Madīnan. He was a trustworthy narrator, and died in the khilāfah of Hishām, as is in *Taqrīb at-tahdhīb*.

cAbd al-Mālik ibn Marwān was one of the khulafāʾ of Banī Umayyah. He was the son of Marwān ibn al-Ḥakam ibn Abi'l-cĀṣ, and he was the first person in Islam to be called cAbd al-Mālik. In his khilāfah there took place events which are mentioned in *Mirʾāt al-jinān* by al-Yāficī and elsewhere. His death, according to what is in *Ḥayāt al-ḥayawān*, was in 76 AH.

cAbd al-Mālik ibn Maysarah – this spelling is from *al-Mughnī* and *Tahdhīb at-tahdhīb* – al-Hilālī Abū Zayd al-cĀmirī the Kūfan. He narrated from Ibn cUmar, Abu'ṭ-Ṭufayl, Ṭāwūs, Sacīd ibn Jubayr and others. Shucbah, Miscar and Manṣūr narrated from him. Ibn Macīn, an-Nasāʾī and al-cIjlī said that he was a trustworthy narrator. Al-Bukhārī mentioned him as one of those who died in the second decade of the second century. He is not the same as cAbd al-Mālik ibn Abī Sulaymān Maysarah al-cAzramī the Kūfan.

cAbd ar-Raḥmān al-Ḥuraqī – by ascription to Ḥuraqah, a clan of Hamdān, but some say of Juhaynah, which is the correct position. Ibn Ḥibbān mentioned him in *ath-Thiqāt* as is in *at-Taqrīb* and *al-Ansāb*.

cAbd ar-Raḥmān ibn cAbd, al-Qāriyy – by ascription to Qārah a sub-clan of Khuzaymah ibn Mudrikah said az-Zurqānī – was the appointee of

ʿUmar in charge of the *bayt al-māl*. Al-ʿIjlī mentions him as one of the trustworthy narrators among the Followers. Al-Wāqidī said different things about him, sometimes saying that he was a Companion, and sometimes that he was a Follower. He died in 88 AH. That is what Ibn Ḥajar said.

ʿAbd ar-Raḥmān ibn ʿAbdullāh, al-Masʿūdī by ascription to Masʿūd the father of ʿAbdullāh ibn Masʿūd. A large group of his descendants have become famous with this name [al-Masʿūdī] as as-Samʿānī mentions, of them ʿAbd ar-Raḥmān ibn ʿAbdullāh ibn Masʿūd al-Hudhalī the Kūfan who narrated from his father, and from ʿAlī, al-Ashʿath ibn Qays and Masrūq, and from whom narrated his two sons al-Qāsim and Maʿn, Sammāk ibn Ḥarb, Abū Isḥāq as-Sabīʿī and others. Yaʿqūb ibn Shaybah said, "He was a trustworthy narrator with few ḥadīth." He died in 79 AH.

ʿAbd ar-Raḥmān ibn ʿAbdullāh ibn ʿUtbah ibn ʿAbdullāh ibn Masʿūd, the Kūfan, al-Masʿūdī (mentioned in ḥadīth 116). This is how he is mentioned in his ascription in *Tahdhīb at-tahdhīb* and *Tadhkirat al-ḥuffāẓ*. What is in *at-Taqrīb* and *al-Ansāb* is, "ʿAbd ar-Raḥmān ibn ʿAbdullāh ibn ʿUtbah ibn Masʿūd narrated from Abū Isḥāq as-Sabīʿī, Abū Isḥāq ash-Shaybānī, al-Qāsim ibn ʿAbd ar-Raḥmān al-Masʿūdī, ʿAlī ibn al-Aqmar, ʿAwn ibn ʿAbdullāh ibn ʿUtbah ibn Masʿūd and others. From him narrated the two Sufyāns, Shuʿbah, Jaʿfar ibn ʿAwn, ʿAbdullāh ibn al-Mubārak and others. Ibn Maʿīn, Ibn al-Madīnī, Aḥmad and others declared him a trustworthy narrator. He became confused at the end of his life, and died in 120 AH."

ʿAbd ar-Raḥmān ibn ʿAbdullāh ibn Abī Ṣaʿṣaʿah al-Anṣārī al-Māzinī, whom an-Nasāʾī and Abū Ḥātim regarded as a trustworthy narrator. He died during the khilāfah of Manṣūr as is in *Isʿāf al-mubaṭṭaʾ* of as-Suyūṭī.

ʿAbd ar-Raḥmān ibn Abī ʿAmrah al-Anṣārī. In the narration of Yaḥyā it [ḥadīth 847] is from Abū ʿAmrah al-Anṣārī. Ibn ʿAbd al-Barr said, "In this way Yaḥyā, Ibn al-Qāsim, Abū Musʿab, and Musʿab az-Zubayrī narrated it. Al-Qa^cnabī, Ma^cn and Yaḥyā ibn Bukayr said that it was from Ibn Abī ^cAmrah. Similarly, Ibn Wahb and ^cAbd ar-Razzāq narrating from Mālik named him ^cAbd ar-Raḥmān and thus removed the problem, for this is the correct position, and this ^cAbd ar-Raḥmān is one of the best of the Followers, as is in *Sharḥ az-Zurqānī* .

^cAbd ar-Raḥmān ibn Abī Bakr aṣ-Ṣiddīq ^cAbdullāh ibn Abī Quḥāfah ^cUthmān. He was ^cĀ^ɔishah's full brother, their mother being Umm Rumān. He accepted Islam in the period of calm after al-Ḥudaybiyyah, and his name had been ^cAbd al-Ka^cbah, so the Messenger of Allah ﷺ name him ^cAbd ar-Raḥmān. He has good merits. It is unknown among the Companions four people each of whom was the son of the one before him and each of whom was a Companions of the Prophet ﷺ and accepted Islam except for Abū Quḥāfah, his son Abū Bakr, his son this ^cAbd ar-Raḥmān and his son Abū ^cAtīq Muḥammad. He had lived in Madīnah, and he refused to pledge allegiance to Yazīd when Mu^cāwiyah sought it. Mu^cāwiyah sent him one hundred thousand dirhams but he returned them and said, "I will not sell my dīn in exchange for my world." He went to Makkah and died suddenly in a place whose name is Ḥabashī, ten miles from Makkah, and then he was carried there and buried in al-Ma^clā. That was in 53 AH according to the majority, but some say 55 AH or 52 AH, as is in *Asad al-ghābah fi ma^crifat aṣ-ṣaḥābah* by Ibn al-Athīr al-Jazarī.

^cAbd ar-Raḥmān ibn Abī Hurayrah. Al-Qārī said, "This ^cAbd ar-Raḥmān has only this ḥadīth [ḥadīth 648 in which he is mentioned as Ibn ^cAbd ar-Raḥmān ibn Abī Hurayrah] in the *Muwaṭṭa^ɔ*." Ibn Ḥibbān mentioned him in *ath-Thiqāt*.

^cAbd ar-Raḥmān ibn Abī Laylā was mujtahid of the generation of the Followers and one of the trustworthy narrators of the ḥadīth scholars.

^cAbd ar-Raḥmān ibn Abī Sa^cīd al-Khudrī was a trustworthy narrator from whom Muslim and the other four [at-Tirmidhī, an-Nasā^ɔī, Ibn Mājah and Abū Dāwūd] narrated. He died in 112 AH as az-Zurqānī said.

ᶜAbd ar-Raḥmān ibn Abi'z-Zinād. He was utterly truthful, a faqīh and Madīnan. His memory changed when he came to Baghdād. He died in 74 AH, as is in *at-Taqrīb*. His father was Abu'z-Zinād ᶜAbdullāh ibn Dhakwān.

ᶜAbd ar-Raḥmān ibn Aflaḥ. He is thus to be found in many copies, and in the copy in the *Sharḥ al-Qārī*. In the *Muwaṭṭa᾽ Mālik* in the version of Yaḥyā, it [ḥadīth 548] is "from Abu'n-Naḍr the mawlā of ᶜUmar ibn ᶜUbaydullāh from Ibn Abī Aflaḥ the mawlā of Abū Ayyūb al-Anṣārī from an Umm Walad of Abū Ayyūb…" Its commentator az-Zurqānī said, "He is ᶜUmar ibn Kathīr ibn Aflaḥ the Madīnan and a trustworthy narrator." What Ibn Ḥajar said in *Taqrīb at-tahdhīb* agrees with him, "ᶜUmar ibn Kathīr ibn Aflaḥ the Madīnan the mawlā of Abū Ayyūb was a trustworthy narrator." As-Suyūṭī said in *Isᶜāf al-mubaṭṭa᾽*, "ᶜUmar ibn Kathīr ibn Aflaḥ the Madīnan the mawlā of Abū Ayyūb narrated from Ibn ᶜUmar, Kaᶜb, Nāfiᶜ, and many others, and from him narrated Ibn ᶜAwn, Yaḥyā al-Anṣārī, and others. An-Nasā᾽ī regarded him as a trustworthy narrator."

ᶜAbd ar-Raḥmān ibn al-Aswad. He was one of those born in the time of the Messenger of Allah ﷺ and it is said that he was a Companion. His father was one of those who mocked the Messenger of Allah ﷺ. That is what Ibn Ḥibbān said in *Kitāb ath-thiqāt*. Ibn al-Athīr al-Jazarī said in *Asad al-ghābah*, "ᶜAbd ar-Raḥmān ibn al-Aswad ibn ᶜAbd Yaghūth ibn Wahb ibn ᶜAbd Manāf ibn Zuhrah al-Qurashī az-Zuhrī had great standing among people. He was the son of the maternal uncle of the Prophet ﷺ. He reached the time of the Prophet ﷺ but it is not authentically established that he saw him or kept his company. Sulaymān ibn Yasār and Marwān and others narrated from him.

ᶜAbd ar-Raḥmān ibn ᶜAwf. One of the ten given the good news of the Garden. He died in 32 AH.

ᶜAbd ar-Raḥmān ibn Ḥanẓalah ibn ᶜAjlān az-Zuraqī, by ascription to Banī Zurayq a clan of the Anṣār. As-Samᶜānī mentioned him. Ibn al-Athīr said in *Jāmiᶜ al-uṣūl,* "ᶜAbd ar-Raḥmān ibn Ḥanẓalah az-Zuraqī related from a mawlā of Quraysh called Ibn Mirs.

ᶜAbd ar-Raḥmān ibn Ḥubāb al-Aslamī al-Anṣārī the Madīnan. Ibn Ḥibbān regarded him as a trustworthy narrator, as is in *at-Taqrīb* and *Isᶜāf al-mubaṭṭa'* of as-Suyūṭī.

ᶜAbd ar-Raḥmān ibn al-Mujabbar ibn ᶜAbd ar-Raḥmān ibn ᶜUmar ibn al-Khattāb. There is in *Sharḥ* al-*Muwaṭṭa* by az-Zurqānī, "ᶜAbd ar-Raḥmān ibn al-Mujabbar, of Quraysh, al-ᶜAdawī narrated from his father and from Sālim. His son Muḥammad and Mālik and others narrated from him. Al-Fallās and others regarded him as a trustworthy narrator." Ibn Mākūlā said, "It is unknown in narration to have ᶜAbd ar-Raḥmān ibn ᶜAbd ar-Raḥmān ibn ᶜAbd ar-Raḥmān, three times in one name, except for this one, because the name of al-Mujabbar was ᶜAbd ar-Raḥmān and his father was ᶜAbd ar-Raḥmān al-Aṣghar."

ᶜAbd ar-Raḥmān ibn al-Qāsim ibn Muḥammad ibn Abī Bakr aṣ-Ṣiddīq the Madīnan the faqīh. Aḥmad and more than one other person regarded him as a trustworthy narrator. He died in Shām in 126 AH. That is how it is in *Isᶜāf al-mubaṭṭa'* of as-Suyūṭī.

ᶜAbd ar-Raḥmān ibn ᶜUthmān ibn ᶜUbaydullāh at-Taymī the Madīnan, was one of the Companions. He was killed along with Ibn az-Zubayr. His son ᶜUthmān, one of the fifth, is trustworthy. That is how it is in *at-Taqrīb*.

ᶜAbd ar-Raḥmān ibn Muḥammad ibn ᶜAbdin al-Qāriyy is ᶜAbd ar-Raḥmān ibn Muḥammad ibn ᶜĀ'ishah ibn ᶜAbdin as is in the *Muwaṭṭa'* of Yaḥyā, and his ascription of al-Qāriyy is to Qārah a clan of the Arabs. He was one of the People of Madīnah and ᶜUmar's appointee to take care of the bayt al-māl. He was a trustworthy narrator from whom ᶜUrwah, Ḥumayd ibn ᶜAbd ar-Raḥmān, and his two sons Ibrāhīm and Muḥammad narrated. He died in 88 AH, as as-Samᶜānī and his father mentioned. He said in *at-Taqrīb*, "Muḥammad ibn ᶜAbdullāh ibn ᶜAbd ar-Raḥmān ibn ᶜAbdin al-Qāriyy the Madīnan is acceptable."[1]

ᶜAbd ar-Raḥmān ibn Sahl ibn Zayd ibn Kaᶜb ibn ᶜĀmir ibn ᶜAdī al-Anṣārī was present at Badr, Uḥud, al-Khandaq and all of the major events, and during his khilāfah ᶜUmar appointed him his governor over Baṣra.

ᶜAbd ar-Raḥmān ibn Yaᶜqūb al-Juhanī al-Madanī. An-Nasāʾī said, "There is no harm in him. His son was al-ᶜAlāʾ Abū Shibl, the utterly truthful Madīnan, as is in *al-Isᶜāf* and *at-Taqrīb*.

ᶜAbd ar-Raḥmān ibn Yazīd ibn Jāriyah al-Anṣārī is Abū Muḥammad the Madīnan whom Ibn Ḥibbān mentioned among the trustworthy narrators of the Followers. It is said that he was born in the lifetime of the Prophet ﷺ, and he died in 93 AH. He witnessed the Farewell Khutbah.

ᶜAbd ar-Raḥmān ibn Yazīd ibn Qays an-Nakhaᶜī – by ascription to Nakhaᶜ, a tribe – Abū Bakr the Kūfan who narrated from his brother al-Aswad ibn Yazīd, his uncle ᶜAlqamah ibn Qays, Ḥudhayfah, Ibn Masᶜūd, Abū Mūsā, ᶜĀʾishah and others, and from whom narrated his son Muḥammad, Ibrāhīm an-Nakhaᶜī, Abū Isḥāq as-Sabīᶜī, Manṣūr and others. Ibn Saᶜd, Ibn Maᶜīn, al-ᶜIjlī and ad-Dāraquṭnī said that he was a trustworthy narrator. He died in 73 AH, but some say 83 AH. Thus it is in *Tahdhīb at-tahdhīb*.

---

[1] Our Shaykh expanded on this at some length in *al-Awjuz* 12/179 when he said, "And that which the author of *at-Taᶜlīq al-Mumajjad* mentions about his biographical notice confuses him with the biographical notice of his grandfather's brother, because the appointee of ᶜUmar died in 88 AH and is ᶜAbd ar-Raḥmān al-Qāriyy, and Imām Malik's birth took place after his death, so how could he narrate from him? On the contrary ᶜAbdullāh ibn ᶜAbdin al-Qāriyy is the brother of ᶜAbd ar-Raḥmān, and this ᶜAbd ar-Raḥmān had been ᶜUmar's appointee ﷺ and the grandfather of Yaᶜqūb ibn ᶜAbd ar-Raḥmān ibn Muḥammad ibn ᶜAbdullāh ibn ᶜAbdin al-Qāriyy, from whom Mālik narrated in the *Muwaṭṭaʾ*. Similarly, ᶜAbd ar-Raḥmān ibn Muḥammad is the one from whom Mālik narrated in this ḥadīth.

ᶜAbd ar-Raḥmān al-Madanī. He saw [the Prophet ﷺ] and was one of the major trustworthy narrators of the Followers. He died in 43 AH, as az-Zurqānī mentioned.

ᶜAbdullāh ibn ᶜAbd ar-Raḥmān ibn Abī Ṣaᶜṣaᶜah, the father of ᶜAbd ar-Raḥmān, was a Follower and a trustworthy narrator, as az-Zurqānī said. An-Nasāʾī declared him a trustworthy narrator, as is in *al-Isᶜāf*.

ᶜAbdullāh ibn ᶜAbd ar-Raḥmān ibn Muᶜammar was Abū Ṭawālah the qāḍī of Madīnah on behalf of ᶜUmar ibn ᶜAbd al-ᶜAzīz. He was a trustworthy narrator and died in 134 AH, as is in *at-Taqrīb*.

ᶜAbdullāh ibn ᶜAbd ar-Raḥmān ibn Yaᶜlā ath-Thaqafī. He said in *at-Taqrīb*, "ᶜAbdullāh ibn ᶜAbd ar-Raḥmān ibn Yaᶜlā ibn Kaᶜb, of Ṭāʾif, Abū Yaᶜlā ath-Thaqafī was utterly truthful."

ᶜAbdullāh ibn ᶜAbdullāh ibn ᶜUmar ibn al-Khattāb of Quraysh al-ᶜAdawī Abū ᶜAbd ar-Raḥmān the Madīnan. He was a Follower who was unanimously agreed to be a trustworthy narrator. He was his father's executor. He died in Madīnah in 105 AH. All of the group of [six ḥadīth collectors] narrated from him apart from Ibn Mājah. That is how it is in *Ḍiyāʾ as-sārī*. In many versions of this book he is [mistakenly mentioned as] ᶜUbaydullāh ibn ᶜAbdullāh.

ᶜAbdullāh ibn ᶜAbdullāh ibn Jābir ibn ᶜAtīk was an Anṣārī Madīnan Follower. Ibn Maᶜīn, Abū Ḥātim and an-Nasāʾī regarded him as a trustworthy narrator, as is in *Isᶜāf al-mubaṭṭaʾ* of as-Suyūṭī.

ᶜAbdullāh ibn ᶜĀmir ibn Rabīᶜah ibn ᶜĀmir ibn Mālik ibn Rabīᶜah ibn Ḥujayr ibn Salāmān ibn Mālik ibn Rabīᶜah ibn Rufaydah ibn ᶜAnz ibn Wāʾil ibn Qāsiṭ al-ᶜAnzī – there is a difference of views about his ascription – Abū Muḥammad. The Prophet ﷺ died when he was four or five years old, and he had a brother older than him called ᶜAbdullāh, and the older brother died as a shahīd on the day of Ṭāʾif. The younger died in 85 AH, but some say 70 AH. Their father was ᶜĀmir and he was an ally of Banī ᶜAdī ibn Kaᶜb, and so for that reason he was called al-ᶜAdawī. He made both hijrahs and was present at Badr and the events after it, and he died in 32 AH but some say 33 AH, or 35 AH. That is how it is in *Jāmiᶜ al-uṣūl* by Ibn al-Athīr al-Jazarī.

ᶜAbdullāh ibn ᶜĀmir. Az-Zurqānī said, "He is Ibn ᶜĀmir ibn Kurayz ibn Ḥabīb ibn ᶜAbd Shams ibn ᶜAbd Manāf of Quraysh. He was born in the lifetime of the Prophet ﷺ, and he was brought to him and he spat lightly upon him." Ibn Ḥibbān said, "He was a Companion, and his maternal uncle's son ᶜUthmān ibn ᶜAffān appointed him governor of Baṣra in 29 AH, and he opened Khurāsān and Kirmān to Islam. He died in Madīnah in 57 AH or 58 AH. His father was a Companion of those who accepted Islam at the Opening [of Makkah to Islam]."

ᶜAbdullāh ibn ᶜAmr ibn ᶜUthmān al-Umawī who was given the honorific name of al-Miṭrāf. He was a noble trustworthy narrator of the Followers and died in Egypt in 96 AH.

ᶜAbdullāh ibn ᶜAmr is Abū ᶜAbd ar-Raḥmān or Abū Muḥammad ᶜAbdullāh ibn ᶜAmr ibn al-ᶜĀṣ ibn Wāʾil ibn Hishām as-Sahmī. There was only eleven years between him and his father and he accepted Islam before his father. He strove and exerted himself in acts of worship and had abundant knowledge and was one of the greatest of the Companions. He died in either 63, 65, 68, 73, or 77 AH in either Makkah, Ṭāʾif, Cairo or Palestine. That is how it is in *Tahdhīb at-tahdhīb* and elsewhere.

ᶜAbdullāh ibn ᶜAyyāsh ibn Abī Rabīᶜah – whose name [Abū Rabīᶜah] was ᶜAmr ibn al-Mughīrah ibn ᶜAbdullāh ibn ᶜUmar ibn Makhzūm of Quraysh and Makhzūm, and he was a Companion and son of a Companion. He was born in Abyssinia. He memorised from the Prophet ﷺ, but he did not narrate from him, but he narrated from ᶜUmar and others. His father was one of the early Muslims, as az-Zurqānī said.

ᶜAbdullāh ibn Abī Bakr ibn Muḥammad ibn ᶜAmr ibn Ḥazm al-Anṣārī the Madīnan, the qāḍī of Madīnah who died in 135 AH, as az-Zurqānī mentioned. His father was Abū Bakr ibn Muḥammad ibn ᶜAmr ibn Ḥazm al-Anṣārī.

A

ᶜAbdullāh ibn Abī Ḥabībah the Madīnan and the mawlā of az-Zubayr ibn al-ᶜAwwām who narrated from Abū Umāmah ibn Sahl ibn Ḥunayf and from ᶜUthmān. Al-Bukhārī mentioned him [narrating] from Ibn Mahdī, and Bukayr ibn al-Ashajj, Mālik, and Abū Ḥanīfah in his *Musnad* narrated from him, "I heard Abu'd-Dardāᵓ ..." and he mentioned the ḥadīth on the merit of someone saying lā ilāha illa'llāh – There is no god but Allah. Ibn al-Ḥidhāᵓ said, "He is one of the men about whom it is sufficient to know that Mālik narrated from them," as is in *Sharḥ az-Zurqānī*

.

ᶜAbdullāh ibn Abī Mulaykah. It is said that his name [Abū Mulaykah's] was Zuhayr at-Taymī the Madīnan, a trustworthy narrator of the Followers. He died in 117 AH, as az-Zurqānī said.

ᶜAbdullāh ibn al-Faḍl. Az-Zurqānī said, "A trustworthy narrator, and one of the narrators of all of them [the major ḥadīth collectors]. He was a lesser Follower of the same generation as az-Zuhrī." As-Suyūṭī said, "An-Nasāᵓī, Abū Ḥātim and Ibn Maᶜīn regarded him as a trustworthy narrator."

ᶜAbdullāh ibn Ḥunayn was a Follower and trustworthy narrator who died during the amirate [khilāfah] of Yazīd. The group [of major ḥadīth narrators] narrated from him, as az-Zurqānī mentioned.

ᶜAbdullāh ibn az-Zubayr. He was Abū Ḥabīb but some say Abū Bakr ᶜAbdullāh ibn az-Zubayr – az-Zubayr was one of the ten given the good news [of the Garden] – ibn al-ᶜAwwām al-Asadī. He was born in the first year of the Hijrah and the Messenger of Allah ﷺ supplicated for him and asked for blessings for him. He fasted and prayed a great deal, and he was pledged allegiance as khalīfah in 64 AH at the end of the epoch of Yazīd ibn Muᶜāwiyah, and the people of Ḥijāz, Yemen, ᶜIrāq and Khurāsān united in obedience to him. Al-Ḥajjāj, the governor on behalf of ᶜAbd al-Mālik ibn Marwān killed him in 72 AH. One of the things he did was to rebuild the Kaᶜbah according to the foundations of Ibrāhīm, upon him and upon our Prophet blessings and peace, as is in *Jāmiᶜ al-uṣūl* and elsewhere.

ᶜAbdullāh ibn Kaᶜb – the mawlā of ᶜUthmān ibn ᶜAffān – al-Ḥimyarī, the Madīnan. He was utterly truthful. Muslim and an-Nasā᾽ī narrated from him, as az-Zurqānī said.

ᶜAbdullāh ibn Masᶜūd. When Ibn Masᶜūd is used unqualifiedly it refers to ᶜAbdullāh ibn Masᶜūd ibn Ghāfil ibn Ḥabīb al-Hudhalī Abū ᶜAbd ar-Raḥmān, one of the first of the forerunners, and one of the great people of knowledge of the Companions. ᶜUmar put him in charge of Kūfa. He died in 32 AH or in the year after in Madīnah, as is in *at-Taqrīb*. He was the keeper of his sandals and his toothstick ﷺ. He emigrated to Ethiopia and was present at Badr and the battles after it. He was appointed qāḍī of Kūfa during the khilāfah of ᶜUmar up until the middle of the khilāfah of ᶜUthmān, and then moved to Madīnah where he died in 32 AH as is in *Asmā᾽ rijāl al-mishkāh*.

ᶜAbdullāh ibn Muḥammad ibn ᶜAlī ibn Abī Ṭālib Abū Hāshim the Madīnan. Ibn Saᶜd and an-Nasā᾽ī regarded him as a trustworthy narrator. He died in 98 AH, as is in *Isᶜāf al-mubaṭṭa᾽* of as-Suyūṭī.

ᶜAbdullāh ibn Muḥammad ibn ᶜAlī ibn Abī Ṭālib al-Hāshimī the Madīnan. Al-ᶜIjlī, Ibn Saᶜd and an-Nasā᾽ī regarded him as a trustworthy narrator. He died in 98 AH. See also his brother al-Ḥasan.

ᶜAbdullāh ibn Muḥammad ibn Abī Bakr aṣ-Ṣiddīq was the brother of al-Qāsim ibn Muḥammad and one of the trustworthy narrators of the Followers. He was killed at al-Ḥarrah in 63 AH.

ᶜAbdullāh ibn Qays ibn Makhramah. Al-ᶜAskarī said, "He saw the Prophet ﷺ." Ibn Abī Khaythamah, al-Baghawī and Ibn Shahīn mentioned him among the Companions. Al-Bukhārī and Ibn Abī Ḥātim mentioned him as one of the great Followers and that his father was a Companion. That is how it is in the *Sharḥ az-Zurqānī*.

ᶜAbdullāh ibn Rāfiᶜ. Ibn Ḥajar said, "ᶜAbdullāh ibn Rāfiᶜ al-Makhzūmī Abū Rāfiᶜ the Madīnan was the mawlā of Umm Salamah, and he was trustworthy."

ᶜAbdullāh ibn Sahl. He and his brother ᶜAbd ar-Raḥmān [see his entry] who began to speak in the presence of the Prophet ﷺ telling the story of the killing of ᶜAbdullāh, and the so the Messenger of Allah ﷺ said to him, "The elder! The elder!", are two sons of Sahl ibn Zayd ibn Kaᶜb ibn ᶜĀmir ibn ᶜAdī al-Anṣārī. As for ᶜAbdullāh he was killed at Khaybar, and it was because of him that the *qasāmah* oath was taken. These two were the two sons of the brother of Ḥuwayyiṣah and Muḥayyiṣah the two sons of Masᶜūd ibn Kaᶜb ibn ᶜĀmir ibn ᶜAdī al-Ḥārithī al-Khazrajī.

ᶜAbdullāh ibn Shaddād is Abu'l-Walīd al-Laythī the Madīnan ᶜAbdullāh ibn Shaddād. Some say his name was Usāmah and Shaddād and his honorific name was Ibn al-Hād, and his name was ᶜAmr and that his honorific name was al-Hādī. Some say his name was Usāmah ibn ᶜAmr ibn ᶜAbdullāh ibn Jābir ibn Bishr. Shaddād narrated from the Prophet ﷺ and he was a Companion. Ibn Saᶜd mentions him as one of those present at al-Khandaq. He had resided in Madīnah but moved to Kūfa. His son ᶜAbdullāh narrated from his father and from Ibn Masᶜūd, Ibn ᶜAbbās, Ibn ᶜUmar, his maternal aunt Asmāʾ bint ᶜUmays the wife of Abū Bakr aṣ-Ṣiddīq, his mother's maternal aunt Maymūnah the Umm al-Muʾminin, ᶜĀʾishah, Umm Salamah and others. From him a large number narrated. Al-ᶜIjlī and al-Khaṭīb said, "He was one of the great Followers and one of their trustworthy narrators." Abū Zurᶜah, an-Nasāʾī and Ibn Saᶜd said he was a trustworthy narrator. Ibn ᶜAbd al-Barr said in *al-Istīᶜāb* that he was born in the time of the Messenger of Allah ﷺ. Al-Maymūnī said, "Aḥmad was asked as to whether he had heard anything from the Prophet ﷺ and he said no." He died in 81 AH, but some say 82 AH. That is how it is in *Tahdhīb at-tahdhīb*.

ᶜAbdullāh ibn Thābit is from Aws, but it is sometimes said that he was from Ẓufr. He died during the life of the Prophet ﷺ. Al-Wāqidī and Ibn al-Kalbī said that he was ᶜAbdullāh ibn ᶜAbdullāh and that both he and his father were Companions. Al-Kalbī said, "He ﷺ buried him in his shirt, and the father lived until the khilāfah of ᶜUmar," as az-Zurqānī mentioned.

ᶜAbdullāh ibn ᶜUmar ibn Ḥafṣ ibn ᶜĀṣim ibn ᶜUmar ibn al-Khattāb Abū ᶜAbd ar-Raḥmān al-ᶜUmarī the Madīnan whom a group of people regard as weak, of them Ibn al-Madīnī, Yaḥyā ibn Saᶜīd and others. Aḥmad, Ibn Maᶜīn and Yaᶜqūb ibn Shaybah regarded him as a trustworthy narrator. He died in Madīnah in 171 AH, as is in *Tahdhīb at-tahdhīb*. I have gone to some lengths in discussing his trustworthiness and that he may be used in proof in my treatise *al-Kalām al-mabrūr fī radd al-qawl al-manṣūr* and in my treatise *as-Saᶜy al-mashkūr fi'r-radd ᶜala'l-madhhab al-maʾthūr* both of which are in examination of the case of visiting the tomb of the Prophet ﷺ.

ᶜAbdullāh ibn ᶜUmar ibn al-Khattāb ibn Nufayl of Quraysh Abū ᶜAbd ar-Raḥmān. He became a Muslim early on while young and emigrated with his father. He took part in al-Khandaq and all of the battles. The Messenger of Allah ﷺ called him the "Right-acting Slave – al-ᶜAbd aṣ-Ṣāliḥ". He has numerous virtues. He died in 73 AH, but some say 74 AH. It is thus in the *Tahdhīb at-tahdhīb* by the Ḥāfiẓ ibn Ḥajar. When one says "Ibn ᶜUmar" one means ᶜAbdullāh ibn ᶜUmar ibn al-Khattāb even though ᶜUmar also had others sons, just as when one says Ibn ᶜAbbās, Ibn Masᶜūd, Ibn az-Zubayr without any qualification one means the one with the name ᶜAbdullāh. His biography is expanded upon in *Tadhkirat al-ḥuffāẓ* by adh-Dhahabī and by others. There is in *Isᶜāf al-mubaṭṭaʾ*, "ᶜAbdullāh ibn ᶜUmar ibn al-Khattāb, of Quraysh, al-ᶜAdawī Abū ᶜAbd ar-Raḥmān the Makkan. He became a Muslim very early on along with his father while he was a youth, and indeed on the contrary it is narrated that he was the first child to be born in Islam. He was regarded too young [to fight] on the day of Uḥud, but he was present at al-Khandaq and the events after it. The Prophet ﷺ said about him, 'He is a right-acting man.' His sons narrated from him: Sālim, Ḥamzah, ʿAbdullāh, Bilāl, ʿUbaydullāh, ʿUmar, and Zayd, and his grandson Muḥammad ibn Zayd, and Abū Bakr ibn ʿUbayd, his mawlā Nāfiʿ, Zayd ibn Aslam, ʿAṭāʾ and a great number of other people. The number of ḥadīth ascribed to him according to Baqī ibn Mukhallad is one thousand six hundred and thirty ḥadīth. He died in 73 AH, but some say 74 AH."

ʿAbdullāh ibn ʿUtbah ibn Masʿūd al-Hudhalī, father of ʿUbaydullāh ibn ʿAbdullāh ibn ʿUtbah [ḥadīth 177] the nephew of ʿAbdullāh ibn Masʿūd whom a large number regarded as a trustworthy narrator and who is one of the great Followers. He died after 70 AH as is in *at-Taqrīb* and elsewhere.

ʿAbdullāh ibn Wāqid ibn ʿAbdullāh ibn ʿUmar al-ʿUmarī the Madīnan. Ibn Ḥibbān regarded him as a trustworthy narrator. He died in 119 AH, as as-Suyūṭī said.

ʿAbdullāh ibn Yazīd al-Anṣārī al-Khatmī was ʿAbdullāh ibn Yazīd ibn Zayd ibn Ḥuṣayn al-Anṣārī al-Khaṭmī – by ascription to Banī Khaṭmah, a tribe of the Anṣār. He was a minor Companion, as is mentioned by al-ʿAynī and others.

ʿAbdullāh ibn Yazīd – the mawlā of al-Aswad ibn Sufyān – al-Makhzūmī al-Maqburī. Aḥmad and Yaḥyā regarded him as a trustworthy narrator. He died in 148 AH, as is mentioned in *al-Isʿāf.*

ʿAbdullāh ibn Zayd ibn ʿĀṣim ibn Kaʿb al-Anṣārī al-Māzinī, the famous Companion. He narrated the description of wuḍūʾ and other things, and he became a shahīd at al-Ḥarrah in 63 AH as is in *Taqrīb at-tahdhīb.*

ʿAbdullāh ibn Zayd ibn ʿĀṣim. He is the grandfather of ʿAmr ibn Yaḥyā. The author of the book *Tahdhīb al-kamāl* said in introduction to ʿAmr ibn Yaḥyā ibn ʿAmmārah that he was the son of the daughter of ʿAbdullāh ibn Zayd ibn ʿĀṣim and that is not the case. It is thus in *Tahdhīb at-tahdhīb* of the Ḥāfiẓ Ibn Ḥajar. ʿAbdullāh ibn Zayd ibn ʿĀṣim is not the ʿAbdullāh ibn Zayds ibn ʿAbd Rabbihī who narrated the ḥadīth on the *adhān,* and whoever says they are the same is deluded. As-Suyūṭī mentions that this ᶜAbdullāh al-Māzinī died in 63 AH.

ᶜAbdullāh aṣ-Ṣunābiḥī. This is how the dominant majority of narrators say [ḥadīth 182]. Muṭarrif and Isḥāq ibn ᶜĪsā aṭ-Ṭabāᶜ said it was Abū ᶜAbdullāh aṣ-Ṣunābiḥī and Ibn ᶜAbd al-Barr said, "That is correct. He is ᶜAbd ar-Raḥmān ibn 'Usaylah one of the Followers and a trustworthy narrator. It is also narrated as… 'I heard the Messenger of Allah ﷺ …' and that is a mistake because aṣ-Ṣunābihī did not meet him. Ḥāfiẓ said in *al-Iṣābah*, 'The apparent meaning of it is that ᶜAbdullāh aṣ-Ṣunābiḥī does not exist about which there are views, for Yaḥyā ibn Maᶜīn said, "ᶜAbdullāh aṣ-Ṣunābiḥī from whom the Madīnans narrate which makes it seem as if he was a Companion." Ibn as-Sakkan said, "It is said that he was a Companion." The narrations of Muṭarrif and aṭ-Ṭabāᶜ from Mālik are contrary to the common view, but Mālik was not alone in that, for on the contrary Ḥafṣ ibn Maysarah followed him in that narrating from Zayd ibn Aslam from ᶜAṭāʾ from ᶜAbdullāh aṣ-Ṣunābiḥī, "I heard the Messenger of Allah ﷺ …" and similarly Zuhayr ibn Muḥammad according to Ibn Mandah, and similarly Muḥammad ibn Jaᶜfar ibn Abī Kathīr and Khārijah ibn Musᶜab, the four narrating from Zayd with it [the rest of the ḥadīth]. Ad-Dāraquṭnī narrated it by way of Ismāᶜīl ibn al-Ḥārith and Ibn Mandah by way of Ismāᶜīl aṣ-Ṣāʾigh from Mālik from Zayd with it [the rest of the ḥadīth], declaring clearly that he [ᶜAbdullāh aṣ-Ṣunābiḥī] had heard it [from the Messenger of Allah ﷺ], as az-Zurqānī mentioned.

ᶜAbīdah ibn Sufyān al-Ḥaḍramī was a trustworthy narrator and was regarded as such by an-Nasāʾī and al-ᶜIjlī, as is in *al-Isᶜāf*.

Abū ᶜAbd ar-Raḥmān [ḥadīth 571]. Ibn ᶜAbd al-Barr said, "There is disagreement about the name of Abū ᶜAbd ar-Raḥmān the shaykh of az-Zuhrī. Some say Sulaymān ibn Yasār, but that is unlikely since he is too important that someone should conceal his name and he should be alluded to by his kunyā. Some said Abu'z-Zinād which is even more unlikely because he did not narrate from Zayd ibn Thābit, he did not see him, and Ibn Shihāb did not narrate from him [in turn]. Some say that he was Ṭāwūs which is more likely to be correct. He would only have concealed his name because Ṭāwūs used to impugn Banī Umayyah and would supplicate against them in his assemblies, but Ibn Shihāb would go to see them and accept their grants. He was asked one time while in the assembly of Hishām, 'Do you narrate from Ṭāwūs?' and he answered the questioner, 'If you had seen Ṭāwūs, you would know that he does not lie,' but he did not answer him as to whether or not he narrated from him. All of this is an indication that Abū ᶜAbd ar-Raḥmān in this ḥadīth [571] is Ṭāwūs."

Abu'l-ᶜĀṣ ibn ar-Rabīᶜ. There is a disagreement about his name. Some said it was Laqīṭ, Mahsham, Hashīm, Muhayshim, but the majority believe it was the first named. He accepted Islam and the Messenger of Allah ﷺ returned Zaynab to him. He died in 12 AH, as is in *al-Istīᶜāb*.

Abu'l-ᶜAwwām al-Baṣrī. Ibn Ḥajar said in *at-Taqrīb,* "ᶜAbd al-ᶜAzīz ibn ar-Rubayyiᶜ al-Bāhilī Abu'l-ᶜAwwām the Baṣran is a narrator trustworthy of the seventh generation. There is in *Tahdhīb at-tahdhīb,* 'ᶜAbd al-ᶜAzīz ibn ar-Rubayyiᶜ al-Bāhilī Abu'l-ᶜAwwām the Baṣran narrated from Abu'z-Zubayr the Makkan and ᶜAṭāᵓ. From him narrated ath-Thawrī, an-Naḍr ibn Shumayl, Wakīᶜ, and Rawḥ ibn ᶜUbādah.' Ibn Maᶜīn said, 'Trustworthy.' Ibn Ḥibbān mentioned him in *ath-Thiqāt*." Some of the leading people of our age think that the Abu'l-ᶜAwwām al-Baṣrī mentioned in this narration is ᶜImrān ibn Dawar Abu'l-ᶜAwwām al-Qaṭṭān al-Baṣrī. He said in *Tahdhīb at-tahdhīb* in his biographical notice abcut him, "He narrated from Qatādah, Muḥammad ibn Sīrīn, Abū Isḥāq ash-Shaybānī and Ḥumayd aṭ-Ṭawīl. From him narrated Ibn Mahdī, Abū Dāwūd aṭ-Ṭayālisī, Abū ᶜAlī al-Ḥanafī and others. ᶜAbdullāh said narrating from his father Aḥmad, "I hope that his ḥadīth are right." Ibn Ḥibbān mentioned him among the trustworthy narrators. Al-Bukhārī said, "Utterly truthful, [but] he imagined [some things]." Al-ᶜIjlī said, "A Baṣran who is trustworthy." (Abridged)

Abū Ayyūb al-Anṣārī's name was Khālid ibn Zayd ibn Kulayb ibn Thaᶜlabah ibn ᶜAbd ibn ᶜAwf ibn Ghanam ibn Mālik ibn an-Najjār. He was present at Badr, Uḥud, al-Khandaq and all the rest of the events with the Messenger of Allah ﷺ and he died in Constantinople in the land of the Byzantines in 50 AH, and it is also said in 51 AH in the amirate of Muᶜāwiyah, as is in *al-Istīᶜāb*.

Abu'l-Baddāḥ ibn ᶜĀṣim ibn ᶜAdī. We have not come across his name and his kunyā is his name. Al-Wāqidī said, "Abu'l-Baddāḥ was an honorific name by which he became generally known, and his kunyā was Abū ᶜAmr." Ibn al-Madīnī and Ibn Ḥibbān said the same. Some said that his kunyā was Abū Bakr, and some said his name was ᶜAdī. He was one of the trustworthy narrators of the Followers. He died in 117 AH but some say 110 AH.

Abū Bakr ibn ᶜAbd ar-Raḥmān. It is said that his name was Muḥammad and it is said that it was Abū Bakr and that his kunyā was Abū ᶜAbd ar-Raḥmān, but the correct position is that his kunyā and his name were one and the same, and he was blind. Al-ᶜIjlī and others regarded him as a trustworthy narrator. He died in 93 AH. That is how it is in *Isᶜāf al-mubaṭṭa᾽* of as-Suyūṭī.

Abū Bakr ibn ᶜAbdullāh an-Nahshalī by ascription to Banī Nahshal a tribe. As-Samᶜānī mentioned him in *al-Ansāb*. In *al-Kāshif* and *at-Taqrīb* there is, "Abū Bakr ibn ᶜAbdullāh an-Nahshalī the Kūfan. It is said that his name was ᶜAbdullāh ibn Qaṭṭāf or Ibn Abī Qaṭṭāf. Some say it was Wahb and some say Muᶜāwiyah. It was utterly truthful and a trustworthy narrator. He died in 166 AH." It is probable that it is him.

Abū Bakr ibn Muḥammad ibn ᶜAmr ibn Ḥazm al-Anṣārī, the qāḍī of Madīnah.

Abū Bakr ibn Sulaymān ibn Abī Ḥathmah was a trustworthy narrator who was knowledgeable in genealogies, but whose own name is not known. Abū Ḥathmah was ᶜAbdullāh ibn Ḥudhayfah al-ᶜAdawī and he was Madīnan, as is in *at-Taqrīb*.

Abū Bakr ibn ᶜUbaydullāh ibn ᶜAbdullāh ibn ᶜUmar ibn al-Khattāb. On this the narrators of the *Muwaṭṭaʾ* are unanimously agreed except for Yaḥyā who said Abū Bakr ibn ᶜAbdullāh ibn ᶜAbdullāh ibn ᶜUmar but that is a mistake, as Ibn ᶜAbd al-Barr said. Az-Zurqānī said, "This Abū Bakr was a Follower who was a trustworthy narrator and who died after 130 AH. His father ᶜUbaydullāh was the full brother of Sālim ibn ᶜAbdullāh." Ibn ᶜAbd al-Barr said about the narration of Yaḥyā ibn Bukayr, "In this narration there is an extra piece which is that it is from his father from Ibn ᶜUmar, but none of the other followers of Mālik agreed with him on that. It is not unknown that Abū Bakr should narrate from his grandfather."

Abū Bakr ibn ᶜUmar according to most of the narrators of the *Muwaṭṭaʾ* and correctly according to Yaḥyā but according to others Ibn ᶜAmr, as Ibn ᶜAbd al-Barr said, and he said, "He is Abū Bakr ibn ᶜUmar ibn ᶜAbd ar-Raḥmān ibn ᶜAbdullāh ibn ᶜUmar ibn al-Khattāb, whose name we have not come across. He was of Quraysh, al-ᶜAdawī and Madīnan and one of the trustworthy narrators." There is only this single ḥadīth [208] ascribed to him in the *Muwaṭṭaʾ* and in the two ṣaḥīḥ books, as is in the *Sharḥ az-Zurqānī*.

Abū Bakr aṣ-Ṣiddīq is Abū Bakr ᶜAbdullāh ibn ᶜUthmān Abū Quḥāfah ibn ᶜĀmir ibn ᶜAmr ibn Kaᶜb who had the honorific surname of al-'Atiq. He was the close friend of the Prophet ﷺ in the cave, who was present with him at all the major events and battles, and he was the first man to accept Islam. He has noted noble qualities. He died in 13 AH. Thus it is in *Asmāʾ rijāl al-mishkāh*.

Abū Bakrah Nufayᶜ ibn al-Ḥārith ath-Thaqafī as is in *Jāmiᶜ al-uṣūl* by Ibn al-Athīr al-Jazarī. In *al-Istīᶜāb* his name is Nufayᶜ ibn Masrūḥ, and it has been said Nufayᶜ ibn al-Ḥārith ibn Kaldah. He came out on the day of Ṭāʾif to the Messenger of Allah ﷺ and accepted Islam along with the slaves of Ṭāʾif, and the Messenger of Allah ﷺ set him free, and so he is counted among his mawlās. He died in Baṣra in 51 AH or 52 AH.

Abū Bujayd al-Anṣārī and then al-Ḥārithī and in another copy he is Ibn Bujayd which agrees with that which is in the *Muwaṭṭaʾ* of Yaḥyā and elsewhere. He is al-Ḥārithī by ascription to Banī Ḥārithah a clan of Khazraj of the Anṣār. His grandmother was Umm Bujayd.

Abu'd-Dardāʾ ʿUwaymir ibn ʿĀmir, but some say ʿĀmir, of Banī Kaʿb ibn al-Khazraj al-Anṣārī al-Khazrajī. There is considerable disagreement on his name and lineage, and he is most known by his kunyā, and ad-Dardāʾ was his daughter. He was a faqīh and an ʿālim, and was present at those battles after Uḥud. He resided in Shām and died in Damascus in 32 AH, but some say 31 AH and some say 34 AH. It is thus in the book *Jāmiʿ al-uṣūl*.

Abū Ghaṭafān. See Ghaṭafān.

Abu'l-Ghayth the mawlā of Abū Muṭīʿ. He mentions in *Tahdhīb at-tahdhīb* and *at-Taqrīb* that he was the mawlā of Ibn Muṭīʿ and that the name of Abu'l-Ghayth was Sālim the Madīnan, whom Ibn Ḥibbān mentions in *ath-Thiqāt,* and whom Ibn Saʿd and Ibn Maʿīn regarded as a trustworthy narrator.

Abū Ḥamzah [ḥadīth 265]. There are many Kūfans called Abū Ḥamzah mentioned in *Tahdhīb at-tahdhīb* and *al-Kāshif* and other books, some of whom are trustworthy narrators and some of whom are weak, and I do not know who the one mentioned here is.

Abu'l-Ḥasan Mūsā ibn Abī ʿĀʾishah. Al-Qārī said in *Sanad al-anām sharḥ Musnad* al-*Imām,* "He was one of the great Followers." There is in *Taqrīb at-tahdhīb,* "Mūsā ibn Abī ʿĀʾishah al-Hamdānī – their mawlā – Abu'l-Ḥasan the Kūfan was a trustworthy narrator and a worshipper." In *al-Kāshif* there is, "Mūsā ibn Abī ʿĀʾishah al-Hamdānī the Kūfan [narrated] from Saʿīd ibn Jubayr and ʿAbdullāh ibn Shaddād. From him narrated Shuʿbah, Jarīr and ʿUbaydah. When he was seen, Allah was remembered."

Abu'l-Ḥasan al-Bazzār is by ascription to the sale of seeds of herbs and leguminous plants, as as-Samᶜānī mentioned. Ibn Ḥibbān said in *Thiqāt at-tābiᶜīn*, "Abu'l-Ḥasan al-Bazzār narrated from ᶜAlī, '[The sale of] animals for animals is not allowable on deferred terms.' Abu'l-ᶜUmays narrated from him."

Abū Ḥāzim is Salamah ibn Dīnār al-Aᶜraj the person who did without the world [zāhid]. He was a trustworthy narrator who narrated a great many ḥadīth, and he used to tell stories in the mosque of Madīnah. He died after 140 AH, as is in *Isᶜāf al-mubaṭṭaʾ* of as-Suyūṭī.

Abū Ḥudhayfah ibn ᶜUtbah ibn Rabīᶜah ibn ᶜAbd Shams ibn ᶜAbd Manāf of Quraysh. His name was Hāshim, but some say Hushm. He was one of the eminent Companions. He emigrated on both emigrations, was present at Badr, Uḥud, al-Khandaq, al-Ḥudaybiyyah and all of the battles, and he was killed as a shahīd on the day of al-Yamāmah at the time of Abū Bakr ﷺ. His wife was Sahlat bint Sahl ibn ᶜAmr and she was of Quraysh and ᶜĀmir. She bore Abū Ḥudhayfah Muḥammad ibn Abī Ḥudhayfah, and to Shamākh ibn Saᶜīd she bore Bukayr ibn Shamākh, and to ᶜAbd ar-Raḥmān ibn ᶜAwf she bore Sālim ibn ᶜAbd ar-Raḥmān, as is in *al-Istīᶜāb*.

Abū Ḥumayd as-Sāʾidī's name was al-Mundhir ibn Saᶜd ibn al-Mundhir, or ibn Mālik. It is said that his name was ᶜAbd ar-Raḥmān or ᶜAmr. He was present at Uḥud and the events after it, and he lived until the beginning of 60 AH, as az-Zurqānī mentioned.

Abū Hurayrah. He is the Ḥāfiẓ of the Companions. There are many disagreements as to his name and his father's name, the weightiest of which according to the majority is ᶜAbd ar-Raḥmān ibn Sakhr. He died in 59 AH, but some say one or two years before that. (*Taqrīb at-tahdhīb*).

Abū Idrīs al-Khawlānī. His name is ᶜĀʾidhu'llāh ibn ᶜAmr al-Qārī, the devout worshipper whose father was a Companion. He was born in the prophetic epoch and is trustworthy and a decisive proof. He died in 80 AH. As-Suyūṭī and others say so.

Abū Isḥāq as-Sabīʿī is ʿAmr ibn ʿAbdullāh ibn ʿUbayd, and some say ʿAlī, as-Sabīʿī by ascription to Sabīʿ a tribe from Hamdān, the Kūfan. He was born two years before the end of ʿUthmān's khilāfah, and he narrated from ʿAlī ibn Abī Ṭālib and al-Mughīrah ibn Shuʿbah – he did see them but he never heard directly from them – and from Sulaymān ibn Ṣurd, Zayd ibn Arqam, al-Barā' ibn ʿĀzib, Jābir ibn Samurah, an-Nuʿmān ibn Bashīr, al-Aswad ibn Yazīd an-Nakhaʿī and his brother ʿAbd ar-Raḥmān ibn Yazīd and his son ʿAbd ar-Raḥmān ibn al-Aswad, Saʿīd ibn Jubayr, al-Ḥārith al-Aʿwar and others. From him narrated ḥadīth his son Yūnus, his grandson Isrā'īl ibn Yūnus and his other grandson Yūsuf ibn Isḥāq, as well as Qatādah, Sulaymān at-Taymī, Misʿar, ath-Thawrī, Sufyān ibn ʿUyaynah and others. Aḥmad, Ibn Maʿīn, an-Nasā'ī, al-ʿIjlī and Abū Ḥātim said he was a trustworthy narrator, and he has many virtues which are set out in detail in *Tahdhīb at-tahdhīb*. His death was in 128 AH, 129 AH, 126 AH or 127 AH, more than one person said. As-Samʿānī said in *Kitāb al-Ansāb* when mentioning as-Sabīʿī "... In Kūfa there is a place well known as as-Sabīʿ because this tribe came to reside there. One of the people of knowledge who is ascribed to this place is Abū Isḥāq as-Sabīʿī whose name is ʿAmr ibn ʿAbdullāh ibn ʿAlī ibn Aḥmad as-Sabīʿī al-Hamdānī who was born in 29 AH during the khilāfah of ʿUthmān, and who saw ʿAlī, Usāmah, Ibn ʿAbbās, al-Barā' ibn ʿĀzib, Zayd ibn al-Arqam, Abū Juḥayfah and Ibn Abī Awfā. Those who narrated from him were al-Aʿmash, ath-Thawrī and Manṣūr. He died in 127 AH. His son was Yūnus ibn Abī Isḥāq."

Abū Isḥāq ash-Shaybānī by ascription to Shaybān a tribe of Bakr ibn Wā'il, which as-Samʿānī mentioned in *al-Ansāb*. He is Sulaymān ibn Abī Sulaymān Abū Isḥāq ash-Shaybānī, their mawlā, the Kūfan,, who narrated from ʿAbdullāh ibn Abī Awfā, Zirr ibn Hubaysh, Abū Bardah ibn Abī Mūsā, ʿAbdullāh ibn Shaddād ibn al-Hād, ʿAbd al-ʿAzīz ibn Rafīʿ, ʿIkrimah,

Ibrāhīm an-Nakhaʿī and others. From him narrated his son Isḥāq, Abū Isḥāq as-Sabīʿī, Ibrāhīm ibn Ṭahmān, Ibn ʿUyaynah and others. Ibn Maʿīn said, "A trustworthy narrator who is a decisive argument." Ibn Abī Ḥātim said, "Utterly truthful, his ḥadīth are good." Al-ʿIjlī said, "He was a trustworthy narrator and one of the major companions of ash-Shaʿbī." Yaḥyā ibn Bakīr said, "He died in 129 AH." Ibn Numayr said, "He died in 139 AH, and his father's name was Fayrūz, and it is said, 'Khāqān,' and some said, 'Mihrān.'" Thus it is in *Tahdhīb at-tahdhīb*.

Abū Jaʿfar Muḥammad ibn ʿAlī ibn al-Ḥusayn ibn ʿAlī ibn Abī Ṭālib, and he is well known as al-Bāqir which he was named because he enlarged his knowledges and sciences a great deal, i.e. he expanded them and deepened them. He heard his father Zayn al-ʿĀbidīn and Jābir ibn ʿAbdullāh, and from him narrated his son Jaʿfar aṣ-Ṣādiq and others. He was born in 56 AH and died in Madīnah in 117 AH, as al-Qārī mentioned in *Sanad al-anām sharḥ Musnad* al-*Imām.*

Abū Jaʿfar al-Qārīʾ. His name was Yazīd ibn al-Qaʿqāʿ and he was Madīnan from Makhzūm, but some have said Jundub ibn Fayrūz, and others that it was Fayrūz. He was a trustworthy narrator. He died in 127 AH, but some have said in 130 AH. Az-Zurqānī.

Abū Jahm whose name was ʿĀmir, but some say ʿUbayd, son of Ḥudhayfah the Companion from Quraysh of those who accepted Islam at the Opening [of Makkah to Islam]. He was one of the shaykhs of Quraysh, and his house was in Balāṭ a place in Madīnah between the mosque and the market. That is what az-Zurqānī said.

Abū Juhaym is ʿAbdullāh ibn Juhaym al-Anṣārī from whom Busr ibn Saʿīd the mawlā of the Ḥaḍramis narrated, from the Messenger of Allah ﷺ concerning the one who passes in front of someone praying. Mālik narrated it from Abu'n-Naḍr the mawlā of ʿUmar ibn ʿUbaydullāh from Busr from Abū Juhaym, without giving his name, because he is more famous by his kunyā. It is said that he was the son of Ubayy ibn Kaʿb's sister, but I have not come across his lineage among the Anṣār. That is how it is in *al-Istī^{c}āb fī aḥwāl al-aṣḥāb* by Ibn ^{c}Abd al-Barr, may Allah have mercy on him.

Abū Kudaynah Yaḥyā ibn al-Muhallab. That is how al-Fattanī spelt it in *al-Mughnī*. He said in *at-Taqrīb*, "Yaḥyā ibn al-Muhallab Abū Kudaynah al-Bajalī the Kūfan is a trustworthy narrator who is utterly truthful and of the most reliable of the Followers."

Abū Laylā was ibn ^{c}Abdullāh ibn ^{c}Abd ar-Raḥmān ibn Sahl al-Anṣārī, but some said that his name was ^{c}Abdullāh. He was a younger Follower who was a trustworthy narrator, as is in *Sharḥ* al-*Muwaṭṭaʾ* by az-Zurqānī. In *Is^{c}āf al-mubaṭṭaʾ* by as-Suyūṭī there is that, "He was Abū Laylā ibn ^{c}Abdullāh ibn ^{c}Abd ar-Raḥmān ibn Sahl al-Anṣārī the Madīnan. Ibn Sa^{c}d said his name was ^{c}Abdullāh ibn Sahl ibn ^{c}Abd ar-Raḥmān and that is how he is iascribed in chains of transmission." In *Taqrīb at-tahdhīb* there is that "He is Abū Laylā ibn ^{c}Abdullāh ibn ^{c}Abd ar-Raḥmān ibn Sahl al-Anṣārī the Madīnan, but some say that his name was ^{c}Abdullāh. He is a trustworthy narrator." Al-Qārī was mistaken when he thought that this Abū Laylā was ^{c}Abd ar-Raḥmān ibn Abī Laylā the Kūfan, who was famous as Ibn Abī Laylā, or his father.

Abū Mā^{c}iz ^{c}Abdullāh ibn Sufyān was one of the notables of the Followers.

Abū Ma^{c}shar's name was Najīḥ ibn ^{c}Abd ar-Raḥmān as-Sindī, a mawlā of Banī Hāshim who was best known by his kunyā. It is said that his name was ^{c}Abd ar-Raḥmān ibn al-Walīd ibn Hilāl in whom there was weakness. At-Tirmidhī said, "He is discussed with respect to his memory." Aḥmad said, "Utterly truthful, but he does not establish the chain of transmission." Ibn ^{c}Adī said, "His ḥadīth are written even though he is weak," as is in *al-Kāshif* and *at-Taqrīb* and *Qānūn al-Mawḍū^{c}āt*.

Abū Mu^{c}āwiyah al-Makfūf i.e. the one whose sight is prevented, meaning he was blind. He is Muḥammad ibn Khāzim aḍ-Ḍarīr the Kūfan who became blind when he was young. He was a trustworthy narrator and the person with the best memory for the ḥadīth of al-A^{c}mash, but he makes mistakes in other people's ḥadīth. He narrated from al-Aᶜmash and Sufyān, and from him narrated Aḥmad, Isḥāq and Ibn Maᶜīn. He died in 195 AH as is mentioned in *al-Kāshif* and *at-Taqrīb*.

Abū Muḥayrīz. In one copy it is Ibn Muḥayrīz, but he is Abū Muḥayrīz ᶜAbdullāh ibn Muḥayrīz ibn Janādah the Makkan from the clan of Abū Maḥdhūrah in whose care he was an orphan. He narrated from Abū Maḥdhūrah, Abū Saᶜīd al-Khudrī, Muᶜāwiyah, ᶜUbādah ibn aṣ-Ṣāmit, Umm ad-Dardā' and others. He was a Follower and a trustworthy narrator and one of the best of the Muslims, as is in *Tahdhīb at-tahdhīb*.

Abū Murrah. His name was Yazīd, but some say ᶜAbd ar-Raḥmān. He was Madīnan and a trustworthy narrator of those from whom everyone narrated as az-Zurqānī mentioned. The Ḥāfiẓ said, "He was the mawlā of Umm Hāniʾ in reality, but he was ascribed to being a mawlā of ᶜAqīl metaphorically because of the least social mixing because he was her brother or because he used to hold to the company of ᶜAqīl a lot."

Abu'l-Muthannā. Adh-Dhahabī said in *al-Kunā*, "Abu'l-Muthannā al-Juhanī [narrated] from Saᶜd and Abū Saᶜīd, and from him [narrated] Ayyūb and Muḥammad ibn Abī Yaḥyā. He was a trustworthy narrator." Ibn ᶜAbd al-Barr said, "I didn't come across his name."

Abu'n-Naḍr the mawlā of ᶜUmar ibn ᶜAbdullāh ibn ᶜUbaydullāh [ḥadīth 903] was Sālim ibn Abī Umayyah. However, Abu'n-Naḍr was the mawlā of ᶜUmar ibn ᶜUbayd ibn Muᶜammar at-Taymī not of ᶜUmar ibn ᶜAbdullāh ibn ᶜUbaydullāh which is very probably a mistake of a copyist. In some copies of this book it is, "Abu'n-Naḍr the mawlā of ᶜUmar ibn ᶜUbaydullāh informed us from ᶜUbaydullāh ibn ᶜAbdullāh ibn ᶜUtbah ibn Masᶜūd …" and this is ṣaḥīḥ. Sālim Abu'n-Naḍr the Madīnan narrated from Anas and as-Sāʾib ibn Yazīd. From him narrated Mālik, al-Layth and the two Sufyāns. Aḥmad and others regarded him as a trustworthy narrator. He died in 129 AH. That is how it is in *Isᶜāf al-mubaṭṭaʾ* of as-Suyūṭī. Az-Zurqānī mentioned him as Sālim ibn Abī Umayyah who was a Follower and a trustworthy narrator.

Abū Qays ᶜAbd ar-Raḥmān ibn Tharwān al-Awdī because of his relationship to Awd a tribe of Madhḥij. It is thus in *al-Ansāb.* In *al-Kāshif* of adh-Dhahabī, "ᶜAbd ar-Raḥmān ibn Tharwān Abū Qays al-Awdī [narrated] from Shurayḥ. Shuᶜbah and ath-Thawrī narrated from him. He is trustworthy." There is in *at-Taqrīb,* "ᶜAbd ar-Raḥmān ibn Tharwān Abū Qays al-Awdī the Kūfan. He is utterly truthful. He died in 120 AH."

Abū Rāfiᶜ was the mawlā of the Messenger of Allah ﷺ. He was first of all the slave of al-ᶜAbbās who gave him to the Messenger of Allah ﷺ who set him free. His name is most reliably recorded as Aslam the Copt, but some have said Ibrāhīm, Thābit, Hurmuz, Sinān, Ṣāliḥ, Yasār, ᶜAbd ar-Raḥmān, Yazīd or Quzmān. He died during the khilāfah of ᶜUthmān but some say during the khilāfah of ᶜAlī which is the correct view. This is as Ibn ᶜAbd al-Barr mentioned in *al-Istīᶜāb.*

Abu'r-Rijāl is Muḥammad ibn ᶜAbd ar-Raḥmān ibn ᶜAbdullāh ibn Ḥārithah ibn an-Nuᶜmān al-Anṣārī. He heard Anas ibn Mālik and his mother, and from him narrated ath-Thawrī and Mālik. He was one of the greatest of the trustworthy narrators. His mother, ᶜAmrah bint ᶜAbd ar-Raḥmān ibn Asᶜad ibn Zurārah, was in ᶜĀ'ishah's lap who brought her up, and from whom she narrated a great deal, and she is one of the famous women of the Followers. Her son, Muḥammad, was given the kunyā Abu'r-Rijāl because he had ten male children, as Ibn al-Athīr and others mentioned.

Abu's-Sā'ib. The Ḥāfiẓ said, "It is said that his name was ᶜAbdullāh ibn as-Sā'ib al-Anṣārī the Madīnan. He was a trustworthy narrator from whom Muslim narrates as well as the Four, and al-Bukhārī in the section on recitation. He was the mawlā of Hishām ibn Zuhrah, but it is also said the mawlā of ᶜAbdullāh ibn Hishām ibn Zuhrah and it is said the mawlā of Banī Zuhrah.

Abū Saᶜīd al-Khudrī whose name was Saᶜd ibn Mālik ibn Sinān ibn ᶜUbayd ibn Thaᶜlabah al-Anṣārī al-Khudrī Khudrah and Khudārah are two small tribes of the Anṣār. He was one of the Ḥāfiẓs who memorised a great deal, and one of the eminent men of intellect. He died in 74 AH. That is how it is in *al-Istīᶜāb*. He was present at every event after Uḥud, and died in Madīnah in 63, 64, or 65 AH, and some say 74 AH. That is how it is in *Jāmiᶜ al-uṣūl*. He is al-Khudrī by ascription to Khudrah who is al-Abjar ibn ᶜAwf ibn al-Ḥārith ibn al-Khazraj. Banū Khudrah are a tribe of the Khazrajī Anṣār and are ascribed to Khudrah. That is how it is in *al-Ansāb* of as-Sama'ni and *Jāmiᶜ al-uṣūl*.

Abū Salamah ibn ᶜAbd ar-Raḥmān ibn ᶜAwf az-Zuhrī. It is said that his name was ᶜAbdullāh, but some say Ismāᶜīl, and others say that his name was his kunyā. Ibn Saᶜd and others regarded him as a trustworthy narrator. He died in Madīnah in 94 AH. That is how it is in *Isᶜāf al-mubaṭṭa*ᵓ of as-Suyūṭī.

Abū Ṣāliḥ Dhakwān as-Sammāk az-Zayyāt the Madīnan. Aḥmad said, "He was a trustworthy narrator, the best of people." Ibn al-Madīnī said, "A trustworthy narrator, firmly established." He died in Madīnah in 101 AH, as is in *Isᶜāf al-mubaṭṭa*ᵓ of as-Suyūṭī. He was the father of Suhayl ibn Abī Ṣāliḥ, and he was a right-acting trustworthy narrator whose ḥadīth are used as proofs." Abū Dāwūd said, "I asked Ibn Maᶜīn, 'Who was the firmly established one in narrating from Abū Hurayrah?' He answered, 'Ibn al-Musayyab, Abū Ṣāliḥ, Ibn Sīrīn and al-Aᶜraj.'" He died in 101 AH as is in *Tahdhīb at-tahdhīb*.

Abū Ṣāliḥ ibn ᶜUbayd the mawlā of as-Saffāḥ – which [as-Saffāḥ] was the honorific name of the first of the khulafāᵓ of Banī al-ᶜAbbās who was ᶜAbdullāh ibn Muḥammad ibn ᶜAlī ibn ᶜAbdullāh ibn al-ᶜAbbās, as we found it expressed in a copy on which al-Qārī had written a commentary. In the *Muwaṭṭa*ᵓ of Yaḥyā there is, "Mālik from Abu'z-Zinād from Busr ibn Saᶜīd from ᶜUbayd ibn Abī Ṣāliḥ the mawlā of as-Saffāḥ…" There is in *Jāmiᶜ al-uṣūl*, "Abū Ṣāliḥ ᶜUbayd ibn Abī Ṣāliḥ the mawlā of as-Saffāḥ was a Follower who narrated from Zayd ibn Thābit and from whom Busr ibn Saᶜīd narrated." In the *Kitāb ath-Thiqāt* by Ibn Ḥibbān there is, "ᶜUbayd ibn Khuzāᶜah is counted as one of the People of Madīnah. He narrated from Zayd ibn Thābit, and Busr ibn Saᶜīd narrated from him."

Abū Shurayḥ al-Kaᶜbī – by ascription to Kaᶜb ibn ᶜAmr a clan of of Khuzāᶜah. His name was Khuwaylid ibn ᶜAmr according to that which is best known, or ᶜAmr ibn Khuwaylid, or Hāni᾿, or Kaᶜb ibn ᶜAmr, or ᶜAbd ar-Raḥmān. He accepted Islam before the Opening [of Makkah to Islam], and he died in Madīnah in 68 AH, as is in *al-Istīᶜāb* and elsewhere.

Abū Sufyān mawlā of Ibn Abī Aḥmad. His name was Wahb says ad-Dāraquṭnī. Others said his name was Quzmān. Ibn Saᶜd said, "He was a trustworthy narrator with few ḥadīth of whom six are narrated." That is how it is *Sharḥ az-Zurqānī* and *at-Taqrīb*.

Abū Suhayl ibn Mālik the paternal uncle of Mālik ibn Anas. His name was Nāfiᶜ. Aḥmad, Abū Ḥātim and an-Nasā᾿ī regarded him as a trustworthy narrator. That is how it is in *Isᶜāf al-mubaṭṭa᾿* of as-Suyūṭī. His father [ḥadīth 135] was Mālik ibn Abī ᶜĀmir, the grandfather of Imām Mālik and one of the trustworthy narrators of the Followers.

Abū Ṭalḥah al-Anṣārī is the husband of Anas' mother Umm Sulaym, and whose name was Zayd ibn Sahl ibn al-Aswad ibn Ḥarām an-Najjārī al-Khazrajī al-Anṣārī, and he is well known by his kunyā. He was one of the great Companions who was present at the pledge of allegiance at al-ᶜAqabah, Badr and those events after. He died in 31 AH, 34 AH, or even 51 AH, as is in *at-Taqrīb*. The Prophet ﷺ said to him that his voice in the army was better than a hundred men. His wife Umm Sulaym bore him a child who died in infancy, and then later ᶜAbdullāh ibn Abī Ṭalḥah in whom they were blessed, and who in turn is the father of Isḥāq. His brothers were ten in number from each of whom knowledge was taken, as Ibn ᶜAbd al-Barr mentioned in *al-Istīᶜāb*.

Abū Thaᶜlabah al-Khushanī is Jurhum but some say Jurthūm ibn Nāshib, and some say Ibn Nāshim, and others say his name was ᶜAmr ibn Jurthūm and even other names. He was one of those who "pledged allegiance under the tree" and the Messenger of Allah ﷺ sent him to his people and they accepted Islam. He resided in Shām and died in the time of Muᶜāwiyah, but some say in the time of ᶜAbd al-Mālik in 75 AH, as is in *al-Istīᶜāb*. His ascription to Khushayn is to the tribe of Quḍāᶜah, as as-Samᶜānī mentioned.

Abū ᶜUbayd the mawlā of ᶜAbd ar-Raḥmān (the Companion, and nephew of ᶜAbd ar-Raḥmān ibn ᶜAwf). His name was Saᶜd ibn ᶜUbayd az-Zuhrī and he was a major Follower found in the main books of ḥadīth, as az-Zurqānī said.

Abū ᶜUbaydah is ibn ᶜAbdullāh ibn Masᶜūd, and he is well known by his kunyā, and the most famous thing is that he has no name other than it, but some say that his name was ᶜĀmir. He was a Kūfan and a trustworthy narrator, one of the great Followers, and he narrated from his father, and from him narrated Isḥāq as-Sabīᶜī and ᶜAmr ibn Murrah. The weightiest view is that it is not sound that he heard from his father. He died in 180 AH, as is in *at-Taqrīb* and *Jāmiᶜ al-uṣūl*.

Abū ᶜUbaydah ibn al-Jarrāḥ was ᶜĀmir ibn ᶜAbdullāh al-Fihrī the 'trusted one' (*Amīn*) of this community [ummah]. ᶜUmar appointed him amīr over Shām.

Abū Umāmah is counted among the Companions because he saw [the Prophet ﷺ], but he did not hear him. His name was Asᶜad, but it is also said that it was Saᶜd. He died in 100 AH. His father was Sahl ibn Ḥunayf the famous Companion who was one of the people of Badr, as az-Zurqānī mentioned.

Abū Wāʾil is Shaqīq ibn Salamah al-Asadī the Kūfan. Adh-Dhahabī said in *Tadhkirat al-ḥuffāẓ*, "*Mukhḍaram* [someone half of whose life was lived in the Jāhiliyyah and half in Islam], magnificent. He narrated from ᶜUmar, ᶜUthmān, ᶜAlī, Ibn Masᶜūd, ᶜĀʾishah and a large body of others. From him narrated al-Aᶜmash, Manṣūr and Ḥuṣayn. It is said that he accepted Islam during the lifetime of the Prophet ﷺ. An-Nakhaᶜī said, 'I reckon Abū Wā᾽il as one of those by whom we are defended.' He died in 82 AH."

Abū Waᶜlah. It is thus found in many copies, but he is Ibn Waᶜlah as in the *Muwaṭṭa᾽* of Yaḥyā. In the narration of Ibn Wahb it is "from Mālik from Zayd from ᶜAbd ar-Raḥmān ibn Waᶜlah as-Sabā᾽ī one of the people of Egypt." In the *Jāmiᶜ al-uṣūl* there is, "Ibn Waᶜlah is ᶜAbd ar-Raḥmān ibn Waᶜlah as-Sabā᾽ī a Follower." As-Samᶜānī said in *al-Ansāb*, "As-Sabā᾽ī is by ascription Sabā who is Saba᾽ ibn Yashḥab ibn Yuᶜrab ibn Qaḥṭān, and they are a group who ascribe themselves to him most of whom are from Egypt." Then later he said, "One of them was ᶜAbd ar-Raḥmān ibn Usmayfaᶜ ibn Waᶜlah who narrated from Ibn ᶜUmar and Ibn ᶜAbbās. He was a noble person in Egypt." In *Isᶜāf al-mubaṭṭa᾽* of as-Suyūṭī, "An-Nasā᾽ī, Ibn Maᶜīn and al-ᶜIjlī regarded him as a trustworthy narrator."

Abū Wāqid al-Laythī from the tribe of Layth ibn Bakr ibn ᶜAbd Manāt ibn ᶜAlī ibn Kinānah ibn Khuzaymah ibn Ilyās ibn Muḍar. There is disagreement about his name, and some say al-Ḥārith ibn ᶜAwf, some say al-Ḥārith ibn Mālik ibn Usayd ibn Jābir ibn ᶜAtūdah ibn ᶜAbd Manāt ibn Sajᶜ ibn ᶜĀmir ibn Layth. Some say he was present at Badr with the Messenger of Allah ﷺ and that he had become a Muslim early on, and some say that he was one of the those who accepted Islam at the the Opening [of Makkah to Islam], but the former is more sound. He died in Makkah in 68 AH as is in *al-Istīᶜāb*.

Abū Yarbūᶜ al-Makhzūmī, and in a copy Ibn Yarbūᶜ which accords with what is in the *Muwaṭṭa᾽* of Yaḥyā, and he is ᶜAbd ar-Raḥmān ibn Saᶜīd ibn Yarbūᶜ al-Makhzūmī Abū Muḥammad the Madīnan who is ascribed to his grandfather, and who is one of the trustworthy narrators of the Followers. He is mentioned in *at-Taqrīb*.

Abū Yūnus the mawlā of ᶜĀ᾽ishah [ḥadīth 349]. Ibn Ḥibbān regarded him as a trustworthy narrator, as as-Suyūṭī said. [Ḥadīth 999] Az-Zurqānī said that he was one of the trustworthy narrators of the Followers. His name is not known.

Abū Ẓabyān. ᶜAbd al-Ghanī and Ibn Mākūlā gave the exact spelling. Al-Ḥāzimī said, "Most of the people of ḥadīth and language [spell it thus] Ẓabyān. His name was Ḥuṣayn ibn Jundub ibn ᶜAmr ibn al-Ḥārith ibn Waḥshī ibn Mālik ibn Rabīᶜah al-Janbī al-Madhḥijī by ascription to the tribe of Madhḥij of the people of Kūfa. He is a famous Follower who heard from ᶜAlī, ᶜAmmār and Usāmah ibn Zayd. From him narrated his son Qābūs and al-Aᶜmash. He died in Kūfa in 90 AH. That is how Ibn al-Athīr al-Jazarī metnioned it in *Jāmiᶜ al-uṣūl.* There is in *Tahdhīb at-tahdhīb,* 'He narrated from ᶜUmar, ᶜAlī, Ibn Masᶜūd, Salman, Usāmah ibn Zayd, ᶜAmmār, Ḥudhayfah, Abū Mūsā, Ibn ᶜAbbās, Ibn ᶜUmar and ᶜĀʾishah, and of the Followers from ᶜAlqamah, Abū ᶜUbaydah ibn ᶜAbdullāh Ibn Masᶜūd, Muḥammad ibn Saᶜd ibn Abī Waqqāṣ and others. From him narrated his son Qābūs, Abū Isḥāq as-Sabīᶜī, Salamah ibn Kuhayl, al-Aᶜmash, and Sammāk ibn Ḥarb. Ibn Maᶜīn, al-ᶜIjlī, Abū Zurᶜah, an-Nasāʾī and ad-Dāraquṭnī said he was trustworthy, and Ibn Ḥibbān mentioned him in *ath-Thiqāt*. Ad-Dāraquṭnī was asked, "Did Abū Ẓabyān meet ᶜUmar and ᶜAlī." He answered, "Yes." Ibn Abī ᶜĀṣim said he died in 89 AH. Ibn Saᶜd and others said he died in 90 AH, and others have said other dates.'"

Abu'z-Zinād is ᶜAbdullāh ibn Dhakwān, and Abu'z-Zinād is his by-name, but he used to be angry at it because of the meanings associated closely with the Fire (*zinād* is a steel for striking fire), but however he has become famous as such because of the excellence of his intelligence. Al-Bukhārī said, "The soundest of the chains of transmission of Abū Hurayrah is: Abu'z-Zinād from al-Aᶜraj from him." Al-Wāqidī said, "He died in 130 AH," and as-Suyūṭī and others say the same.

Abu'z-Zubayr Muḥammad ibn Muslim ibn Tadrus the Makkan, the mawlā of Ḥakīm ibn Ḥizām, one of the Followers of Makkah. He heard Jābir, ᶜĀʾishah, Ibn ᶜAbbās, Ibn ᶜUmar and others. Mālik narrated from him, the two Sufyāns, Ayyūb as-Sakhtiyānī, Ibn Jurayj, Shuᶜbah, ath-Thawrī, and others. He was a ḥāfiẓ who was a trustworthy narrator. He died in 128 AH. That is how it is in *Jāmiʿ al-uṣūl* and *al-Kāshif*. He narrated from Jābir, Ibn ʿUmar, Ibn ʿAbbās, Ibn az-Zubayr and ʿĀʾishah, and from him narrated Mālik, Abū Ḥanīfah, Shuʿbah and the two Sufyāns. Ibn al-Madīnī, Ibn Maʿīn and an-Nasāʾī regarded him as a trustworthy narrator. He died in 128 AH, as is in *Isʿāf al-mubaṭṭaʾ* of as-Suyūṭī.

ʿAfīf ibn ʿAmr ibn al-Musayyab as-Sahmī. I read in the handwriting of adh-Dhahabī, "It is not known who he was, i.e. ʿAfīf ibn ʿAmr. Ibn Ḥibbān mentions him in *ath-Thiqāt*, and an-Nasāʾī said he was a trustworthy narrator. That is how it is in the *Tahdhīb at-tahdhīb* of Ibn Ḥajar.

Aḥmad [ḥadīth 159].[2]

ʿĀʾishah bint Abī Bakr aṣ-Ṣiddīq the wife of the Prophet ﷺ and the most beloved of his wives to him. Her mother was Umm Rumān bint ʿĀmir ibn ʿUwaymir ibn ʿAbd Shams. He married her when she was a girl of six or seven, two years before the Hijrah according to Abū ʿUbaydah. Others said it was three years before the Hijrah. He took up residence with her in Madīnah when she was nine. Az-Zuhri said, "If ʿĀʾishah's knowledge were to be gathered together with the knowledge of all of the wives of the Messenger of Allah ﷺ and the knowledge of all women, the knowledge of ʿĀʾishah would be superior." That is how it is in *al-Istīʿāb* of Ibn ʿAbd al-Barr. Abu'ḍ-Ḍuḥā said that Masrūq said, "I saw the major Companions of the Prophet ﷺ asking her about the shares of inheritance." ʿAṭāʾ said, "ʿĀʾishah was the person with the most fiqh and the most knowledgeable of people." She died in 57 AH, but some say 58 AH, on the 17th of Ramaḍān. That is how it is in *al-Istīʿāb fi aḥwāl al-aṣḥāb* by Ibn ʿAbd al-Barr.

ʿĀʾishah bint Qudāmah ibn Maẓʿūn was of Quraysh and Jumaḥ. She was a Companion as was her mother Rīṭah bint Sufyān who was one of those who pledged allegiance [at al-ʿAqabah], as is in *al-Istīʿāb*.

---

[2] Aḥmad ibn Mihrān an-Nasawī a companion of Imām Muḥammad who narrated the *Muwaṭṭaʾ* from him according to Dr Taqī ad-Dīn an-Nadwī.

ᶜĀᵓishah bint Ṭalḥah of Quraysh. She was extremely beautiful. A trustworthy narrator from whom the six have narrated as az-Zurqānī mentioned.

ᶜAlāᵓ (or al-ᶜAlāᵓ) ibn ᶜAbd ar-Raḥmān ibn Yaᶜqūb. His name was Abū Shibl. He was a Madīnan and utterly truthful as is in *al-Isᶜāf* and *at-Taqrīb*. He was the mawlā of al-Ḥuraqah, a tribe of Hamdān as Ibn Ḥibbān said or from Juhaynah as ad-Dāraquṭnī said, which is correct, as is in *Ansāb as-Samᶜānī*. He died in 132 AH. Ibn Ḥibbān mentioned him in *ath-Thiqāt* as is in *at-Taqrīb* and *al-Ansāb*.

Al-ᶜAlāᵓ ibn al-Ḥārith. Al-ᶜAlāᵓ ibn al-ᶜAlāᵓ ibn al-Ḥārith ibn ᶜAbd al-Wārith al-Ḥaḍramī Abū Wahb or Abū Muḥammad of Damascus. He narrated from Makḥūl, az-Zuhrī and ᶜAmr ibn Shuᶜayb. From him narrated al-Awzāᶜī, ᶜAbd ar-Raḥmān ibn Thābit ibn Thawbān and others. Ibn Maᶜīn, Ibn al-Madīnī and Abū Dāwūd said he was a trustworthy narrator. Abū Ḥātim said, "He was one of the best of the companions of Makḥūl." Duḥaym said, "He has priority over the companions of Makḥūl, and he is a trustworthy narrator who died in 136 AH." That is how it is in *Tahdhīb at-tahdhīb*.

ᶜAlī ibn ᶜAbd ar-Raḥmān al-Muᶜāwī. Abū Zurᶜah and an-Nasāᵓī regarded him as a trustworthy narrator as as-Suyūṭī said. He was called al-Muᶜāwī by ascription to Banī Muᶜāwiyah a part of the Anṣār. He was a Madīnan Follower who was a trustworthy narrator, and from whom Muslim and Abū Dāwūd narrated, as az-Zurqānī said.

ᶜAlī ibn Abī Ṭālib ᶜAbd Manāf ibn ᶜAbd al-Muṭṭalib of Quraysh al-Hāshimī the son of the paternal uncle of the Messenger of Allah ﷺ and the husband of the daughter of the Messenger of Allah ﷺ. He grew up with the Prophet ﷺ and prayed with him as the first of people [to do so]. He was present at all the battles and expeditions apart from Tabūk [for which we was left in charge of Madīnah]. He has many merits, and was killed as a shahīd on the night of the Jumuᶜah thirteen days before the end of Ramaḍān in 40 AH in Kūfa, as is in *Asad al-ghābah* and *Isᶜāf al-mubaṭṭa᾽* of as-Suyūṭī, by which we know that the narration of Ibrāhīm an-Nakhaᶜī from him was mursal because he did not live at that time.

ᶜAlī ibn Ḥusayn ibn ᶜAlī ibn Abī Ṭālib who is Zayn al-ᶜĀbidīn the son of Sayyid ash-Shuhadā᾽ al-Ḥusayn.

ᶜAlqamah ibn Qays ibn ᶜAbdullāh ibn Mālik ibn ᶜAlqamah Abū Shabil an-Nakhaᶜī the Kūfan paternal uncle of al-Aswad an-Nakhaᶜī. He was born during the lifetime of the Messenger of Allah ﷺ and narrated from ᶜUmar, ᶜUthmān, ᶜAlī, Saᶜd, Ḥudhayfah, Abu'd-Dardā᾽, Ibn Masᶜūd, Abū Mūsā, Khālid ibn al-Walīd, Salamah ibn Yazīd al-Juᶜfī, ᶜĀ᾽ishah and others. From him narrated his brother's son ᶜAbd ar-Raḥmān ibn Yazīd ibn Qays an-Nakhaᶜī, his sister's son Ibrāhīm ibn Yazīd an-Nakhaᶜī, Ibrāhīm ibn Suwayd an-Nakhaᶜī, ᶜĀmir ash-Shaᶜbī, Abū Wā᾽il Shaqīq ibn Salamah, Abū Isḥāq as-Sabīᶜī and others. Ibn al-Madīnī said, "The people who knew ᶜAbdullāh ibn Masᶜūd best were ᶜAlqamah, al-Aswad, ᶜUbaydah and al-Ḥārith." Ibn Maᶜīn, Shuᶜbah, Ibn Sīrīn and others said he was a trustworthy narrator and praised him. He is one of the most significant companions of Ibn Masᶜūd. He died in 161 AH, but some say 162, 163, 165, 172 and even after that.

ᶜAlqamah ibn Wā᾽il ibn Ḥujr al-Ḥaḍramī al-Kindī the Kūfan narrated from his father, al-Mughīrah ibn Shuᶜbah and Ṭāriq ibn Suwayd. From him narrated his brother ᶜAbd al-Jabbār, his nephew Saᶜīd, ᶜAmr ibn Murrah, Sammāk ibn Ḥarb and others. Ibn Ḥibbān mentioned him in *ath-Thiqāt*. Ibn Saᶜd said, "He was a trustworthy narrator with few ḥadīth." Al-ᶜAskarī quoted Ibn Maᶜīn as saying, "ᶜAlqamah narrating from his father is a mursal ḥadīth." Thus it is in *Tahdhīb at-tahdhīb*.

ᶜAlqamah [ḥadīth 26]. Al-Qārī said in his *Sharḥ*, "He is ᶜAlqamah ibn Abī ᶜAlqamah [see ḥadīth 85] Bilāl the mawlā of ᶜĀ᾽ishah the mother of the mu᾽minūn, and he narrated from Anas ibn Mālik and from his own mother. Mālik ibn Anas and others narrated from him." He is a Madīnan. There are other men known as ᶜAlqamah from among the scholars of Kūfa, one of whom may be one of Imām Muhammad's narrators for one of his narrations. (See ʿAlqamah ibn Qays, and see p. 222 of *at-Taʿlīq al-mumajjad,* from Dār al-Qalam of Damascus, for a detailed discussion). His mother [ḥadīth 390] was the freed slave [*mawlāh*] of ʿĀʾishah ؓ [see Marjānah].

Amāmah bint Zaynab is Amāmah bint Abi'l-ʿĀṣ ibn ar-Rabīʿ ibn ʿAbd al-ʿUzzā ibn ʿAbd Shams ibn Manāf. Her mother was Zaynab the daughter of the Messenger of Allah ﷺ. She was born in the time of the Messenger of Allah ﷺ and he used to love her, and probably carried her on his neck in the prayer. ʿAlī ibn Abī Ṭālib married her after Fāṭimah. When ʿAlī was killed, al-Mughīrah ibn Nawfal ibn al-Ḥārith ibn ʿAbd al-Muṭṭalib married her to whom she bore Yaḥyā, and then she died while married to him. Some said that she did not give birth neither while married to ʿAlī nor to al-Mughīrah, and that Zaynab has no posterity, as is in *al-Istīʿāb*.

Al-Aʿmash is derived from al-ʿAmash which is expressive of weaksightedness and the fact that tears used to stream from his eyes because of an illness. The person who is famous with this name is Sulaymān ibn Mihrān al-Asadī al-Kāhilī – their mawlā – Abū Muḥammad the Kūfan whose origin was in Ṭabaristān, but who was born in Kūfa. He narrated from Anas, but it is not established that he heard from him directly, and from Ibn Abī Awfā, Abū Wāʾil, Qays ibn Abī Ḥāzim, ash-Shaʿbī, an-Nakhaʿī and others. From him narrated Abū Isḥāq as-Sabīʿī, Shuʿbah, the two Sufyāns and others. Ibn Maʿīn said he was a trustworthy narrator. An-Nasāʾī said he was a firm trustworthy narrator. Ibn ʿAmmār said, "There is not among the narrators of ḥadīth anyone more firm than al-Aʿmash, and Manṣūr is also firm except that al-Aʿmash had more knowledge than he did about the chain of transmission." He died in 147 AH, but some say 146 AH, and there is a lengthy biographical notice on him in *Tahdhīb at-tahdhīb.*

ʿĀmir ash-Shaʿbī is ʿĀmir Sharāḥīl ash-Shaʿbī, by ascription to Shaʿb a sub-clan of Hamdān, the Kūfan, and he was one of the great Followers. He was a faqīh, poet and he narrated from one hundred and fifty

Companions. He died in 104 AH, and some say in 109 AH as is mentioned by as-Samᶜānī. He mentioned in *Tahdhīb at-tahdhīb*, "Makḥūl said, 'I have never seen anyone more discerning (*afqah*, lit. with more fiqh) than him.' Ibn ᶜUyaynah said, 'The people after the Companions were ash-Shaᶜbī in his time and ath-Thawrī in his time.' Ibn Maᶜīn said, 'When ash-Shaᶜbī narrates a ḥadīth from a man whom he names, then he is a trustworthy narrator.' He and Abū Zurᶜah said that he was a trustworthy narrator. Ibn Ḥibbān mentioned him in *ath-Thiqāt*. Al-ᶜIjlī said, 'Ash-Shaᶜbī could hardly relate a mursal ḥadīth that was not ṣaḥīḥ.' Abū Dāwūd said, 'The mursal ḥadīth of ash-Shaᶜbī are preferable to me than the mursal ḥadīth of an-Nakhaᶜī.'" (Abridged)

ᶜĀmir ibn Saᶜd ibn Abī Waqqāṣ az-Zuhrī the Madīnan. Ibn Ḥibbān regarded him as a trustworthy narrator. He died in 96 AH, but some say in 103 AH, as is in *Isᶜāf al-mubaṭṭaʾ*.

ᶜAmmār ibn Yāsir is Abu'l-Yaqẓān ᶜAmmār ibn Yāsir ibn ᶜĀmir ibn Mālik ibn Kinānah. He accepted Islam and emigrated [both] to Abyssinia and Madīnah. He was present at Badr and all the battles. The Messenger of Allah ﷺ said to him, "The rebellious party will kill you," and he was killed at Ṣiffīn while with ᶜAlī ؓ. The people with Muᶜāwiyah killed him in 37 AH. That is how it is in *Jāmiᶜ al-uṣūl* by Ibn al-Athīr al-Jazarī.

ᶜAmr ibn al-Ḥārith ibn Yaᶜqūb ibn ᶜAbdullāh al-Anṣārī – he was their mawlā – Abū Umayyah the Egyptian. Ibn Maᶜīn, an-Nasāʾī and many others regarded him as a trustworthy narrator. He died in 148 AH, but some say 149 AH, as is in *al-Isᶜāf*.

ᶜAmr ibn ash-Sharīd ath-Thaqafī aṭ-Ṭāʾifī Abu'l-Walīd of Ṭāʾif was one of the trustworthy narrators of the Followers, as az-Zurqānī and others said.

ᶜAmr ibn ᶜUbaydullāh al-Anṣārī whom Ibn Ḥibbān mentioned in the book *ath-Thiqāt* in which he named his father as ᶜUbayd. He said, "He was from Banī al-Ḥārith ibn al-Khazraj of the people of Madīnah. He narrated from Ibn ᶜAbbās and from him narrated Mālik ibn Anas and Sulaymān ibn Bilāl."

ᶜAmr ibn al-ᶜĀṣ ibn Wāʾil as-Sahmī the Companion. He became a Muslim in the year of al-Ḥudaybiyyah, and was made the amīr of Egypt twice. He died there around 40 AH, and some say after 50 AH. That is how az-Zurqānī mentioned it in his *Sharḥ* al-*Muwaṭṭa*. ᶜAmr ibn al-ᶜĀṣ accepted Islam at the hands of an-Najāshī (the Negus) before accompanying the Prophet ﷺ and so an riddle was made of him when it was said, "He was a Companion who narrated many ḥadīth and who accepted Islam at the hands of a Follower."

ᶜAmr ibn Ḥazm ibn Zayd ibn Lawdhān al-Anṣārī was present at al-Khandaq and the events after that. He was the governor for the Messenger of Allah ﷺ in Najrān. He died after 50 AH, as az-Zurqānī said. He was Abū Muḥammad, but some say Abu'ḍ-Ḍāḥik, ᶜAmr ibn Ḥazm ibn Zayd ibn Lawdhān ibn ᶜAmr ibn ᶜAbd ᶜAwf ibn Ghanam ibn Mālik ibn an-Najjār al-Anṣārī al-Khazrajī an-Najjārī the Madīnan. The first event at which he was present with the Messenger of Allah ﷺ was al-Khandaq, and the Messenger of Allah ﷺ appointed him as the governor of Najrān in the Yemen, and he sent along with him a writing in which there were the obligatory shares of inheritances and the Sunnahs, the amounts paid in zakāh, retaliations and compensatory payments due for damages done and wounds inflicted, and compensatory payments due for homicide. This writing of his is famous. Abū Dāwūd, an-Nasāʾī and others narrated it in separate bits, and the most complete narration of it is by an-Nasāʾī in the chapter on compensatory payments for homicides and injuries. He died in Madīnah in 51 AH or 53 AH or 54 AH according to the different views, as is in *Tahdhīb an-Nawawī*.

ᶜAmr ibn Ḥusayn was a trustworthy narrator. Muslim and at-Tirmidhī narrated from him, and he was ᶜAmr ibn Ḥusayn ibn ᶜAbdullāh al-Jumaḥī – their mawlā – Abū Qudāmah, the Makkan, as is in *at-Taqrīb*.

ᶜAmr ibn Muḥammad ibn Zayd. It is thus in some copies and in some authentic copies it is ᶜUmar ibn Muḥammad ibn Zayd who is ᶜUmar ibn Muḥammad ibn Zayd ibn ᶜAbdullāh ibn ᶜUmar ibn al-Khattāb al-ᶜAdawī the Madīnan who resided in ᶜAsqalān, and who narrated from his father and grandfather Zayd, and from his father's paternal uncle Sālim, and Zayd ibn Aslam, Nāfiᶜ and others. From him narrated Shuᶜbah, Mālik, the two Sufyāns and Ibn al-Mubārak. Ibn Saᶜd said, "He was a trustworthy narrator with few ḥadīth." ᶜAbdullāh ibn Aḥmad said [narrating] from his father, "A shaykh who is a trustworthy narrator, and in whom there is no harm." Ḥanbal said [narrating] from Aḥmad, "A trustworthy narrator." Ibn Maᶜīn, al-ᶜIjlī, Abū Dāwūd and Abū Ḥātim said the same. Most of his residence was in Shām and then he went to Baghdād and then Kūfa, where they learnt from him. He died after his brother Abū Bakr, and Abū Bakr died after the uprising of Muḥammad ibn ᶜAbdullāh ibn Ḥasan which occurred in 145 AH. That is how it is in the *Tahdhīb at-tahdhīb*.

ᶜAmr ibn Murrah [ḥadīth 107] is Abū ᶜAbdullāh ᶜAmr ibn Murrah ibn ᶜAbdullāh ibn Ṭāriq ibn al-Ḥārith ibn Salamah ibn Kaᶜb ibn Wā᾽il ibn Jamal ibn Kinānah ibn Nājiyah ibn Murād al-Jamalī al-Murādī the blind Kūfan. He narrated from ᶜAbdullāh ibn Abī Awfā, Abū Wā᾽il, Saᶜīd ibn al-Musayyab, ᶜAbd ar-Raḥmān ibn Abī Laylā, ᶜAmr ibn Maymūn al-Awdī, Saᶜīd ibn Jubayr, Musᶜab ibn Saᶜd, an-Nakhaᶜī and others. From him narrated his son ᶜAbdullāh, Abū Isḥāq as-Sabīᶜī, al-Aᶜmash, Manṣūr, Ḥuṣayn ibn ᶜAbd ar-Raḥmān, ath-Thawrī, Shuᶜbah and others. Ibn Maᶜīn said that he was a trustworthy narrator. Abū Ḥātim said that he was utterly truthful and a trustworthy narrator. Shuᶜbah said, "He had the most knowledge among them. I have not seen anyone of the people of ḥadīth who did not conceal gaps in his chains of transmission (*tadlīs*) except for Ibn ᶜAwn, ᶜAmr ibn Murrah and Misᶜar. There was no one in Kūfa more beloved to me than him nor was there anyone better." Ibn Ḥibbān mentioned him in the book *ath-Thiqāt* and he said, "He was one of the Murjiʾah[3]." He died in 116 AH. Ibn Numayr and Yaᶜqūb ibn Sufyān regarded him as a trustworthy narrator. That is how it is in the *Tahdhīb at-tahdhīb*, *al-Kāshif* and *Tadhkirat al-ḥuffāẓ*. Al-Qārī wrongly considered him a Companion.

ᶜAmr ibn Rāfiᶜ al-ᶜAdawī – he was their mawlā – and he is acceptable. He mentions him in *at-Taqrīb*.

ᶜAmr ibn Shuᶜayb ibn Muḥammad ibn ᶜAbdullāh ibn ᶜAmr ibn al-ᶜĀṣ of Quraysh. It very often occurs in the books of ḥadīth that we find "ᶜAmr ibn Shuᶜayb from his father from his grandfather…" Ibn al-Qaṭṭān said, "When trustworthy narrators transmit from him then he is a trustworthy narrator by whom one may use in proof." Al-Bukhārī said, "I saw Aḥmad ibn Ḥanbal, ᶜAlī ibn al-Madīnī, Isḥāq ibn Rāhwayh and people in general of our companions using the ḥadīth of ᶜAmr ibn Shuᶜayb from his father from his grandfather in proof. None of the Muslims abandon him." He died in 118 AH, as is in *Isᶜāf al-mubaṭṭaʾ* of as-Suyūṭī.

ᶜAmr ibn Sulaym az-Zuraqī, by ascription to Banī Zurayq, ibn ᶜAbd Ḥārithah, a clan of the Anṣār, as as-Samᶜānī mentioned.

ᶜAmr ibn ᶜUbaydullāh al-Anṣārī. Ibn Ḥibbān mentioned him in *Kitāb ath-Thiqāt* but he called his father ᶜUbayd, and he said, "He was from Banī al-Ḥārith ibn al-Khazraj of the people of Madīnah. He narrated from Ibn ᶜAbbās and from him Mālik ibn Anas and Sulaymān ibn Bilāl narrated."

ᶜAmrah bint ᶜAbd ar-Raḥmān ibn Saᶜd ibn Zurārah was in the room of ᶜĀʾishah who brought her up, and she narrated many ḥadīth from her and from others. A large number narrated from her among them Yaḥyā ibn Saᶜīd al-Anṣārī, his son Abu'r-Rijāl Muḥammad ibn ᶜAbd ar-Raḥmān ibn Ḥārithah and Abū Bakr ibn Muḥammad ibn ᶜAmr ibn Ḥazm. She died in 103 AH and is one of the famous female Followers. That was

[3] The *Murjiʾah* are the dialectical opposite of the Khawārij. They are noted for taking a lax position on points of ᶜaqīdah on which the Khawārij were severe.

what Ibn al-Athīr al-Jazarī said in *Jāmiᶜ al-uṣūl*. She died before the end of the first century or just after as as-Suyūṭī mentioned.

ᶜAmrah bint Ḥazm was the paternal aunt of the grandfather of ᶜAbdullāh ibn Abī Bakr and so she was called his paternal aunt metaphorically speaking. She was a companion of old from whom Jābir the Companion narrated.

Anas ibn Mālik was the servant of the Messenger of Allah ﷺ and he served him for ten years. The Messenger of Allah ﷺ supplicated for him saying, "O Allah increase him in wealth and in children, and enter him into the Garden." He died in 102 AH, but some say 92 AH, having passed one hundred years in age. That is how it is in *Isᶜāf al-mubaṭṭa' bi rijal* al-*Muwaṭṭa'* of as-Suyūṭī.

Anas ibn Sīrīn is Abū Mūsā Anas the son of Sīrīn al-Anṣārī the Madīnan the mawlā of Anas, and he is the brother of Muḥammad ibn Sīrīn. He narrated from his master, Ibn ᶜAbbās, Ibn ᶜUmar and a large group. From him narrated Shuᶜbah and the two Ḥammāds. Ibn Maᶜīn declared him to be a trustworthy narrator as well as an-Nasā'ī, Abū Ḥātim, Ibn Saᶜd and al-ᶜIjlī. He died in 118 AH, but it is also said 125 AH. That is how it is in *Tahdhīb at-tahdhīb.*

ᶜAqīl ibn Abī Ṭālib ibn ᶜAbd al-Muṭṭalib ibn Hishām of Quraysh whose kunyā was Abū Yazīd. We have narrated that the Prophet ﷺ said to him, "Abū Yazīd, I love you with two loves: a love because of your kinship to me, and a love because of what I know of my uncle's love for you." ᶜAqīl went to Baṣra and then Kūfa, and then later he went to Shām. He died in the time of Muᶜāwiyah. That is in *al-Istīᶜāb.*

Al-Aᶜraj. As-Samᶜānī said in *al-Ansāb,* "Al-Aᶜraj... is because of an ascription to *al-ᶜaraj* – natural lameness. The one who is well known by this name is Abū Ḥāzim ᶜAbd ar-Raḥmān ibn Hurmuz ibn Kaysān al-Aᶜraj the mawlā of Muḥammad ibn Rabīᶜah ibn al-Ḥārith ibn ᶜAbd al-Muṭṭalib who narrated from Abū Hurayrah and from whom az-Zuhrī and Abu'z-Zinād narrated in turn."

Arqam ibn Shuraḥbīl. His names are as al-Fattanī spelt them out. He said in *Tahdhīb at-tahdhīb,* "Arqam ibn Shuraḥbīl the Kūfan al-Awdī narrated from Ibn ᶜAbbās and Ibn Masᶜūd. From him narrated Abū Isḥāq and his brother Hudhayl ibn Shuraḥbīl. Abū Zurᶜah said he is trustworthy, and Aḥmad ibn Ḥanbal used his ḥadīth as definitive proofs. Ibn ᶜAbd al-Barr said, 'It is a ṣaḥīḥ ḥadīth and Arqam is a tremendous trustworthy narrator.' Al-ᶜUqaylī transmitted with a sound chain of transmission from Abū Isḥāq as-Sabīᶜī that he said, 'Hudhayl and Arqam were two sons of Shuraḥbīl one of the best companions of Ibn Masᶜūd.'" (Abridged)

Asīd was the father of Khālid ibn Asīd and of his brother ᶜAttāb ibn Asīd whom the Messenger of Allah ﷺ apppointed governor of Makkah in the year of the Opening [of Makkah to Islam].

ᶜĀṣim ibn ᶜAdī ibn al-Jadd ibn al-ᶜIjlān ibn Ḥārithah al-Quḍāᶜī al-Anṣārī was one of the Companions who was present at Uḥud and other events. He lived for 125 years, as is in *Sharḥ az-Zurqānī* .

ᶜĀṣim ibn Kulayb ibn Shihāb ibn al-Majnūn al-Jarmī the Kūfan. He narrated from his father, Abū Buraydah, ᶜAlqamah ibn Wāʾil ibn Ḥujr and others. From him narrated Shuᶜbah, the two Sufyāns and others. An-Nasāʾī regarded him as a trustworthy narrator and Ibn Maᶜīn. Abū Dāwūd said, "He was one of the best of the people of Kūfa." Ibn Ḥibbān mentioned him among the trustworthy narrators, and he gave the date of his death as 137 AH. His father Kulayb ibn Shihāb was a trustworthy narrator. That is how it is in *Tahdhīb at-tahdhīb* and *al-Kāshif.* In *al-Ansāb* of as-Samᶜānī there is, "Al-Jarmī by ascription to Jarm a Yemeni tribe from whom of the Companions there was Shihāb ibn al-Majnūn al-Jarmī the grandfather of ᶜĀṣim ibn Kulayb."

Aslam the father of Zayd ibn Aslam was a mawlā of ᶜUmar and a trustworthy narrator who had lived half of his life in the Jāhiliyyah and half of it in Islam. He died in 87 AH. That is how it is in *Isᶜāf al-mubaṭṭaʾ* of as-Suyūṭī and other works.

Asmā᾽ bint ᶜUmays was the sister of Maymūnah the wife of the Prophet ﷺ and of Umm al-Faḍl the wife of al-ᶜAbbās, and she was the sister of their sisters by the same mother who were nine in number, and some say ten. Asmā᾽ was one of the emigrants to the land of the Ethiopians along with her husband Jaᶜfar ibn Abī Ṭālib to whom she bore Muḥammad, ᶜAbdullāh and ᶜAwn. Then she emigrated to Madīnah. When Jaᶜfar was killed Abū Bakr aṣ-Ṣiddīq married her and she bore him Muḥammad. When he died, ᶜAlī married her and she bore him Yaḥyā, as is in *al-Istīᶜāb*.

Al-Aswad ibn Yazīd ibn Qays an-Nakhaᶜī by ascription to the tribe of Nakhaᶜ in Kūfa. He narrated from Abū Bakr, ᶜUmar, Ḥudhayfah, Bilāl, ᶜĀ᾽ishah, Abū Maḥdhūrah, Abū Mūsā and Ibn Masᶜūd and was a faqīh who did without the world and who was the one of his companions who issued fatwās. Abū Isḥāq as-Sabīᶜī, Ibrāhīm an-Nakhaᶜī – his sister's son – Abū Bardah ibn Abī Mūsā and a group narrated from him. Aḥmad, Yaḥyā, Ibn Saᶜd and al-ᶜIjlī regarded him as a trustworthy narrator. He died in Kūfa in 75 AH, but some say 74 AH, says Ibn Abī Shaybah. That is how it is in *Tahdhīb at-tahdhīb*.

ᶜAṭā᾽ [ḥadīth 264] is either Ibn Abī Rabāḥ the Makkan or Ibn Yasār the Madīnan, and in some editions it is found to be like that "ᶜAṭā᾽ ibn Yasār…".

ᶜAṭā᾽ ibn Abī Rabāḥ Aslam Abū Muḥammad of Quraysh, the Makkan. He narrated from ᶜĀ᾽ishah, Ibn ᶜAbbās, Abū Hurayrah and others. Al-Awzāᶜī, Ibn Jurayj, Abū Ḥanīfah, al-Layth and others narrated from him. He is trustworthy, a faqīh, of high standing. He died in 114 AH according to the well known position. It is thus in adh-Dhahabi's *al-Kāshif* and Ibn Hajar's *at-*Taqrīb.

ᶜAṭā᾽ ibn Yasār Abū Muḥammad al-Hilālī the Madīnan the mawlā of Maymūnah the mother of the mu᾽minūn. He was an eminent trustworthy narrator who was given to worship of Allah and who delivered admonitory discourse. He was one of the Followers, and he died in 94 AH, but some say after that. That is how it is in *at-Taqrīb*. ᶜAṭā᾽ ibn Yasār al-Hilālī Abū

Muḥammad the Madīnan narrated from Ibn Masᶜūd, Zayd and Ibn ᶜUmar. From him narrated Abū Ḥudhayfah, Zayd ibn Aslam and others. Ibn Maᶜīn, Abū Zurᶜah, an-Nasāʾī and others regarded him as a trustworthy narrator. He died in 94 AH, but some say 103 AH. That is how it is in *Isᶜāf al-mubaṭṭaʾ* of as-Suyūṭī. He was the brother of Sulaymān, ᶜAbdullāh and ᶜAbd al-Mālik who were all mawlās of Maymūnah the mother of the muʾminūn who wrote contracts with all of them that they could purchase their freedom, and all of them took knowledge from her, but ᶜAṭāʾ was the one with the most ḥadīth. All of them were trustworthy narrators, as az-Zurqānī mentioned.

ᶜAṭāʾ ibn Yazīd al-Laythī the Madīnan was one of the trustworthy narrators of the Followers. He died in 105 or 107 AH. His father's name was Yazīd. That is how it is in *Isᶜāf al-mubaṭṭaʾ* of as-Suyūṭī and *at-Taqrīb*. In some copies it is: Zayd.

ᶜAṭāʾ al-Khurāsānī is ᶜAṭāʾ ibn Abī Muslim Maysarah, and some say ᶜAbdullāh al-Khurāsānī Abū ᶜUthmān the mawlā of al-Muhallab ibn Abī Ṣufrah according to the most well known position, but some say a mawlā of Hudhayl. He was originally from the city of Balkh in Khurāsān, and he resided in Shām. He was born in 50 AH, and he was an eminent person knowledgeable of the Qurʾān and an ᶜālim whom Ibn Maᶜīn regarded as a trustworthy narrator. He died in 135 AH. Al-Bukhārī recorded him among the weak narrators because of the narration of al-Qāsim ibn ᶜĀṣim ibn al-Musayyab that he called him [ᶜAṭāʾ] a liar, but Ibn ᶜAbd al-Barr refuted that because the narration of someone such as al-Qāsim cannot be used against the likes of ᶜAṭāʾ, who was one of the eminent people of knowledge, as az-Zurqānī mentioned.

ᶜAtīk ibn al-Ḥārith ibn ᶜAtīk is acceptable he said in *at-Taqrīb*.

Ayyūb ibn Abī Tamīmah Kaysān as-Sakhtiyānī Abū Bakr the Baṣran. He was called as-Sakhtiyānī by ascription to the sale of *sakhtiyān*, which are sheepskins, which Ayyūb used to sell and from which he gained this ascription, as is mentioned in *Ansāb as-Samᶜānī* and its abridgement by

Ibn al-Athīr known as *al-Lubāb.* As for what as-Suyūṭī said in his abridement *Lubb al-Lubāb* that it was spelt as *sikhtiyān,* then ᶜAbdullāh ibn Sālim the Baṣran and Makkan has previously written about drawing attention to that. Ayyūb saw Anas and narrated from ᶜAṭā', ᶜIkrimah, ᶜAmr ibn Dīnār, al-Qāsim ibn Muḥammad, ᶜAbd ar-Raḥmān ibn al-Qāsim and others. From him narrated Shuᶜbah, the two Ḥammāds, the two Sufyāns, Mālik, Ibn ᶜUlayyah and others. Ibn Saᶜd said, "He was a trustworthy narrator who was firmly established in ḥadīth, was comprehensive, with great knowledge, and he was a decisive proof and a just witness." Abū Ḥātim said, "He was a trustworthy narrator, and one does not ask about the like of him." ᶜAlī said, "The most firmly established in [narrating] from Nāfiᶜ are Ayyūb, ᶜUbaydullāh and Mālik." The trustworthy narrators have said a great deal in praise of him as he explained at length in *Tahdhīb al-kamāl* and *Tahdhīb at-tahdhīb* and *Tadhkirat al-ḥuffāẓ*. He died in 131 AH.

Ayyūb ibn Ḥabīb the mawlā of Saᶜd ibn Abī Waqqāṣ. Adh-Dhahabī said in *al-Kāshif,* "Ayyūb ibn Ḥabīb the Madīnan [narrated] from Abu'l-Muthannā, and from him narrated Mālik and Fulayḥ. An-Nasā'ī regarded him as a trustworthy narrator."

Ayyūb ibn ᶜUtbah Abū Yaḥyā the qāḍī of al-Yamāmah from Banī Qays ibn Thaᶜlabah. There is disagreement as to whether he is trustworthy or weak. Ibn Ḥajar said in *Tahdhīb at-tahdhīb,* "He narrated from Yaḥyā ibn Abī Kathīr, ᶜAṭā', Qays ibn Ṭalq al-Ḥanafī and a large body of people. Those who narrated from him included Abū Dāwūd aṭ-Ṭayālisī, Aswad ibn ᶜĀmir, Muḥammad ibn al-Ḥasan, Aḥmad ibn Yūnus and others. Ḥanbal said, narrating from Aḥmad, 'Weak.' He said in another place, 'Trustworthy except for the fact that he does not get the ḥadīth of Yaḥyā ibn Abī Kathīr straight.' Ad-Dūrī said, narrating from Ibn Maᶜīn, 'Abū Kāmil said, "He is not anything."' Ibn al-Madīnī, al-Jūzajānī, ᶜAmr ibn ᶜAlī and Muslim said, 'Weak,' and ᶜAmr added, 'He had a bad memory, although he was a truthful person.' Al-ᶜIjlī said, 'His ḥadīth are [to be] written down, but he is not strong.' Al-Bukhārī said, 'According to them he is flabby.' (Abridged)" Ayyūb's shaykh was Qays ibn Ṭalq, one of the Followers, an utterly truthful man. His father was Ṭalq ibn ᶜAlī ibn al-Mundhir, al-Ḥanafī by relationship to the tribe of Banū Ḥanīfah, Abū ᶜAlī al-Yamāmī and is reckoned among the Companions. Ibn Ḥajar mentioned him in *Taqrīb at-tahdhīb*, as did others.

ᶜAzīz ibn Marthad. He mentioned in *Ansāb as-Samᶜānī* after mention of al-Mashriqī by ascription to Mashriq a clan of Hamdān, "The person who is best known with this ascription is ᶜUrayb ibn Marthad al-Mashriqī al-Hamdānī who narrated statements from the Followers which stop short at them [*maqṭūᶜ*], and from whom narrated ᶜAbd al-Jabbār ibn al-ᶜAbbās ash-Shibāmī." (Abridged) From this it is known that the name of the shaykh of ᶜAbd al-Jabbār was ᶜUrayb and not ᶜAzīz.

B

Al-Barāʾ ibn ʿĀzib ibn al-Ḥārith ibn ʿAdī al-Anṣārī of Aws. The first encounter at which he was present was the Trench (al-Khandaq). He went to reside in Kūfa where he died at the time of Musʿab ibn az-Zubayr in 72 AH as is in *Jāmiʿ al-uṣūl*.

Al-Barāʾ ibn Qays. Ibn Ḥibbān said in *Thiqāt at-tābiʿīn*, "Al-Barāʾ ibn Qays Abū Kabshah the Kūfan is counted as one of the people of Kūfa, and he narrated from Ḥudhayfah and Saʿd, and other people narrated from him.

Bashīr ibn Saʿd Abu'n-Nuʿmān ibn Thaʿlabah al-Anṣārī al-Khazrajī. He was a major Companion who was present at Badr, and he was the father of an-Nuʿmān ibn Bashīr. He became a shahīd at ʿAyn at-Tamr, as az-Zurqānī mentioned.

Bashīr ibn Yasār al-Ḥārithī the Madīnan. Ibn Maʿīn declared him a trustworthy narrator. Ibn Saʿd said, "He was an old shaykh who had reached most of the Companions of the Messenger of Allah ﷺ, but who had few ḥadīth."

Bilāl ibn al-Ḥārith ibn ʿĀṣim ibn Saʿīd ibn Qurrah ibn Khalādah ibn Thaʿlabah Abū ʿAbd ar-Raḥmān al-Muznī. He came to the Prophet ﷺ in the deputation from Muzaynah in 5 AH, and he carried the banner for Muzaynah on the day of the the Opening [of Makkah to Islam]. Later he lived in Baṣra, and he died in 60 AH in the last days of Muʿāwiyah ؓ as is in *Asad al-ghābah fī maʿrifat aṣ-ṣaḥābah* by ʿIzz ad-Dīn ibn Muḥammad who is better known as Ibn al-Athīr al-Jazarī.

Bilāl ibn Rabāḥ, the Ethiopian, the muʾadhdhin whose mother was Ḥamāmah. He became a Muslim and emigrated early on. He was the mawlā of Abū Bakr ؓ and he was present at Badr and all of the major battles and military expeditions. He died in Damascus in 17 or 18 AH, but some say 20 AH, or even 21 AH when he was just over sixty years old. Some say he died in Madīnah, but that is wrong. That is how it is in *al-Iṣābah* and other works such as the *Tahdhīb* of an-Nawawī.

Bishr [ḥadīth 159]. This chain of transmission is thus in some copies, but in others it is Bisr, and in some Muḥammad ibn Bishr. Until now, I have not been able to find out who he is or who his shaykh Aḥmad is so that I could find out from the books on the narrators whether or not they are trustworthy, and perhaps Allah will graciously bestow that knowledge on me later.[4]

Bukayr ibn ᶜAbdullāh ibn al-Ashajj [ḥadīth 160]. This name is thus in numerous copies, but in the *Muwaṭṭaʾ* of Yaḥyā it is narrated as "from Mālik from someone he regarded as a trustworthy narrator", who was al-Layth ibn Saᶜd, as ad-Dāraquṭnī mentioned. Manṣūr ibn Salamah said, "This is one of those Mālik narrated from al-Layth as Ibn ᶜAbd al-Barr mentioned. Most of what is in the books of Mālik from Bukayr, then his companions say that he took it from the books of Bukayr which he had taken from Makhramah his son and investigated. However, this does not apply here, as az-Zurqānī mentioned. Bukayr was a trustworthy narrator from whom the six narrated. He died in 120 AH or after, said az-Zurqānī .

Bukayr ibn ᶜĀmir was Abū Ismāᶜīl Bukayr – the diminutive form – ibn ᶜĀmir al-Bajalī the Kūfan about whom there is disagreement. He narrated from Qays ibn Abī Ḥāzim, Abū Zurᶜah ibn ᶜAmr ibn Jarīr and others. From him narrated ath-Thawrī, Wakīᶜ and others. Aḥmad once said, "His ḥadīth are fine, there is no harm in him," but another time [he said], "He is not strong." An-Nasāʾī regarded him as weak, as did Abū Zurᶜah and Ibn Maᶜīn. Ibn ᶜAdī said, "He was not given much to narration, and his narrations are few, but I have not found any texts of his which are to be rejected, and he is one of those whose ḥadīth are written down." Ibn Saᶜd and al-Ḥākim said that he was a trustworthy narrator,

[4] He is Bishr ibn Mūsā al-Asadī according to Dr Taqī ad-Dīn an-Nadwī.

and Ibn Ḥibbān mentions him in *ath-Thiqāt*. That is how it is in *Tahdhīb at-tahdhīb*.

Bushayr ibn Yasār al-Ḥārithī al-Anṣārī, their mawlā, the Madīnan. Ibn Ma^{c}īn said that he was a trustworthy narrator. Ibn Sa^{c}d said, "He was a great shaykh and a faqīh who lived to meet most of the Companions, but he narrated few ḥadīth." An-Nasāʾī said he was a trustworthy narrator. Thus it is in *Tahdhīb at-tahdhīb*.

Busr ibn Miḥjan was an utterly truthful Follower as is said in *at-Taqrīb*. Aṭ-Ṭaḥāwī mentioned from Abū Dāwūd al-Barnasī from Aḥmad ibn Ṣāliḥ al-Miṣrī that he said, "I asked a large number as to who was his [Miḥjan's] son of the group of men around him and no two of them differed in saying that he was Bishr, as ath-Thawrī said." Abū ^{c}Umar said, "Mālik said Busr and ath-Thawrī said Bishr, but most people take the position that Mālik took." That is how it is in *al-Istī^{c}āb fī aḥwāl al-aṣḥāb* by Ibn ^{c}Abd al-Barr. For his father see Miḥjan ad-Dīlī.

Busr ibn Sa^{c}īd was a Madīnan worshipper and a trustworthy narrator who was a ḥāfiẓ, and a narrator whom everyone used, said az-Zurqānī .

D

Aḍ-Ḍaḥḥāk ibn Khalīfah ibn Thaᶜlabah al-Anṣārī al-Ashhalī. He was present at the engagement of Banī an-Naḍīr and there are no narrations from him. He was suspected of being a hypocrite, then later he turned in tawbah and became right acting, as is in *al-Iṣābah* and elsewhere.

Aḍ-Ḍaḥḥāk ibn Qays ibn Khālid ibn Wahb al-Fihrī Abū Anīs the well known amīr was a Companion, and he was killed in the events of Marj Rāhiṭ in 64 AH as az-Zurqānī and others said.

Aḍ-Ḍaḥḥāk ibn Sufyān ibn ᶜAwf ibn Kaᶜb ibn Abī Bakr ibn Kilāb ibn Rabīᶜah al-Kilābī al-ᶜĀmirī aḍ-Ḍibābī, by ascription to Ḍibāb ibn ᶜĀmir ibn Ṣaᶜṣaᶜah and also to a place in Kūfa, but however as aḍ-Ḍabābī it is by ascription to Ḍabāb a clan of Banī al-Ḥārith and of Quraysh. He is counted as one of the people of Madīnah. He had resided in Najd and the Prophet ﷺ appointed him as ruler over those of his people who accepted Islam. He was one of the bravest of the Companions, as Ibn al-Athīr mentioned in Jāmiᶜ al-uṣūl.

Ḍamrah ibn Saᶜīd ibn Abī Ḥannah ᶜAmr ibn Ghaziyah al-Anṣārī al-Māzinī by ascription to Māzin ibn an-Najjār a tribe of the Anṣār. He narrated from Abū Saᶜīd, Anas and a number of others, and from him narrated Mālik, Ibn ᶜUyaynah and they regarded him as a trustworthy narrator, as is in *al-Kāshif* by adh-Dhahabī. His father Saᶜīd was Ibn Abī Ḥannah. Ibn Maᶜīn, an-Nasāʾī, Abū Ḥātim and al-ᶜIjlī said he was a trustworthy narrator. Ibn Ḥibbān mentioned him in *ath-Thiqāt*. Thus it is in *Tahdhīb at-tahdhīb*.

The daughter of Zayd ibn Thābit. They mention that Zayd had the following daughters: Ḥasanah, ᶜAmrah, Umm Kulthūm and others, but I have only seen narations from Umm Kulthūm the wife of Sālim ibn ᶜAbdullāh ibn ᶜUmar.

Dāwūd ibn al-Ḥuṣayn. Ibn Maᶜīn regarded him as a trustworthy narrator. He died in 135 AH, as is in *al-Isᶜāf*.

Dāwūd ibn Qays al-Farrā' – by ascription to the sale and sewing of furs as is mentioned by as-Samcānī. Abū Sulaymān Dāwūd ibn Qays al-Farrā' ad-Dabbāgh the Madīnan who narrated from as-Sā'ib ibn Yazīd, Zayd ibn Aslam, Nāfic the mawlā of Ibn cUmar, Nāfic ibn Jubayr ibn Muṭcim and others. From him narrated the two Sufyāns, Ibn al-Mubārak, Yaḥyā al-Qaṭṭān, Wakīc and others. Ash-Shāficī, Aḥmad Ibn Macīn, Abū Zurcah, Abū Ḥātim, an-Nasā'ī, as-Sājī, Ibn al-Madīnī and others regarded him as a trustworthy narrator, and the author of *at-Tahdhīb* and *Tahdhīb at-tahdhīb* mentioned their expressions. He died in the khilāfah (*wilāyah*) of Abū Jacfar.

Dāwūd ibn Sacd ibn Qays [ḥadīth 128]. It is thus in some copies and in some other copies it is Dāwūd ibn Qays who is probably the aforementioned Dāwūd ibn Qays al-Farrā' the Madīnan.

Dhu'l-Yadayn – "Two Hands". Ibn Ḥajar said, "Most take the position that his name was al-Khirbāq relying upon what occurred in the ḥadīth of cImrān ibn Ḥuṣayn according to Muslim whose wording is, 'A man stood up to him, said to be al-Khirbāq in whose hands there was length...' This is what those do who unite together the ḥadīth of Abū Hurayrah with the ḥadīth of cImrān, which is the weightiest in my view, even though Ibn Khuzaymah and those who follow him inclined to regard them as separate [ḥadīth about different men]. What made them do that was the difference that occurs in the development [of the ḥadīth], because in the ḥadīth of Abū Hurayrah there is that the salām was after two [rakcahs] and in the ḥadīth of cImrān that it was after three."

F

Al-Faḍl ibn cAbbās was the brother of cAbdullāh ibn cAbbās the son of the maternal uncle of the Messenger of Allah ﷺ. He had many merits, and he was present at Ḥunayn and the Farewell Ḥajj. He went to Shām after the death of the Prophet ﷺ, and died in the precincts of Jordan in the plague of cAmawās in 18 AH, but some say in 15 AH and other things, as Ibn al-Athīr said.

Al-Faḍl ibn Ghazwān as is found in a number of authentic copies, but what is in *Tahdhīb at-tahdhīb* and *at-Taqrīb* and *al-Kāshif* is that he was al-Fuḍayl – with the diminutive – ibn Ghazwān Ibn Jarīr aḍ-Ḍabbī – their mawlā – Abu'l-Faḍl the Kūfan, who narrated from Sālim, Nāfic, cIkrimah and others, and from whom narrated his son Muḥammad, ath-Thawrī, Ibn al-Mubārak, Wakīc and others. Ibn Ḥibbān mentioned him in *ath-Thiqāt* and Aḥmad, Ibn Macīn, Yacqūb ibn Sufyān and others regarded him as a trustworthy narrator. He was killed after 140 AH.

Father of Muḥammad ibn cAbdullāh ibn cAbd ar-Raḥmān ibn Abī Ṣacṣacah was cAbdullāh ibn cAbd ar-Raḥmān ibn Abī Ṣacṣacah. An-Nasā'ī regarded him as a trustworthy narrator, as is in *Iscāf al-mubaṭṭa'* of as-Suyūṭī.

Father of Sacīd al-Maqburī. His name was Kaysān ibn Sacīd al-Maqburī the Madīnan, Abū Sacīd the mawlā of Umm Sharīk. He was a firmly established trustworthy narrator and he died in 100 AH. His son Sacīd al-Maqburī was a Madīnan and a trustworthy narrator, and he died around 120 AH, or a little before or after that, as is in *at-Taqrīb*.

Father of cUbaydullāh ibn cAbdullāh ibn cUtbah [ḥadīth 177] see cAbdullāh ibn cUtbah ibn Mascūd al-Hudhalī.

Al-Furaycah bint Mālik ibn Sinān. Ibn cAbd al-Barr said in *al-Istīcāb,* "Al-Furaycah bint Mālik ibn Sinān was the sister of Abū Sacīd al-Khudrī. She is called al-Fāricah. She was present at the Pledge of Allegiance of Riḍwān. Her mother was Ḥabībah bint cAbdullāh ibn Salūl, and Zaynab bint Kaᶜb ibn ᶜUjrah narrated her ḥadīth respecting the residence granted to the widow, which most of the fuqahāʾ of the different lands use.

G

Ghaṭafān ibn Ṭarīf is mentioned in present editions, but in the *Muwaṭṭa*ʾ of Yaḥyā it is mentioned that it is "from Mālik from Dāwūd ibn al-Ḥuṣayn that Abū Ghaṭafān ibn Ṭarīf al-Murrī informed him that his father..." Abū Ghatafan's name was Saᶜd and he was a Follower who was a trustworthy narrator. His father Ṭarīf was also one of the Followers, and his ascription – al-Murrī – is to Murr which is a tribe, as as-Samᶜānī mentioned.

The grandmother [ḥadīth 179] of Isḥāq ibn ᶜAbdullāh ibn Abī Ṭalḥah see Umm Sulaym.

H

Habbār ibn al-Aswad ibn al-Muṭṭalib ibn Asad ibn ᶜAbd al-ᶜUzzā of Quraysh the famous Companion who accepted Islam after the Opening [of Makkah to Islam], and who made good his Islam, as Ibn al-Athīr mentioned in *Asad al-ghābah fi maᶜrifat aṣ-ṣaḥābah*.

Ḥabīb. He said in *Tahdhīb at-tahdhīb*. "Ḥabīb ibn ᶜUbayd ar-Raḥabī Abū Ḥafṣ al-Ḥimṣī narrated from al-ᶜIrbāḍ ibn Sāriyah, al-Miqdām ibn Maᶜdīkarib, Jubayr ibn Nufayr, Bilāl ibn Abi'd-Dardā᾽ and others. From him narrated Jarīr ibn ᶜUthmān, Thawr ibn Yazīd, and Muᶜāwiyah ibn Ṣāliḥ. An-Nasā᾽ī said that he was a trustworthy narrator. He said, "And Ḥabīb ibn ᶜUbayd said, 'I reached to meet seventy men of the Companions.'" Al-ᶜIjlī said that he was a trustworthy narrator, and Ibn Ḥibbān mentioned him among the trustworthy narrators." (Abridged)

Ḥafṣah bint ᶜUmar ibn al-Khattāb whom the Messenger of Allah ﷺ married in 3 AH according to most of them but Abū ᶜUbaydah said in 2 AH. She died in 41 AH, but some say in 39 AH. Thus it is in *al-Isᶜāf*.

Al-Ḥajjāj ibn ᶜAmr ibn Ghaziyyah al-Anṣārī al-Māzinī the Madīnan was a Companion. He was present at Ṣiffīn along with ᶜAlī r, as is in *Sharḥ az-Zurqānī*.

Al-Ḥakam ibn ᶜUyaynah. He is thus recorded in the present copies, but the correct position according to *Mushtabih an-nisbah, Tahdhīb at-tahdhīb*, and its *Taqrīb* and elsewhere is that he was al-Ḥakam ibn ᶜUtaybah Abū Muḥammad al-Kindī – their mawlā – the Kūfan who narrated from a large number of Companions and Followers. Ibn ᶜUyaynah, Ibn Mahdī, Aḥmad, Yaḥyā ibn Saᶜīd, al-ᶜIjlī, Ibn Saᶜd and others regarded him as a trustworthy narrator. Al-Bukhārī said in *at-Tārīkh al-kabīr*, "Al-Qaṭṭān said, 'Shuᶜbah said, "Al-Ḥakam [narrating] from Mujāhid is [from a] writing unless he said, 'I heard…'"'" Ibn Ḥibbān said in *ath-Thiqāt*, "He used to omit mentioning gaps in his chains of transmission (*tadlīs*)." He died in 113 AH, 114 AH or a year after that.

H

Ḥakīm ibn Ḥizām ibn Khuwaylid ibn Asad ibn ᶜAbd al-ᶜUzzā of Quraysh and Asad. He was the son of the brother of Khadījah, the mother of the believers (Umm al-Muᵓminīn). He accepted Islam on the day of the Opening [of Makkah to Islam] and became a Companion when he was 74 years old. He lived up until 54 AH or after.

Ḥammād ibn Abī Sulaymān Muslim al-Ashᶜarī Abū Ismāᶜīl the Kūfan the faqīh. Muᶜammar said, "I have seen no one more discerning in fiqh than these: az-Zuhrī, Ḥammād and Qatādah." Ibn Maᶜīn said, "Ḥammād is trustworthy." Abū Ḥātim said, "Utterly truthful." Al-ᶜIjlī said, "From Kūfa and trustworthy, he was the most discerning in fiqh of Ibrāhīm's companions." An-Nasāᵓī, "Trustworthy, except for the fact that he was one of the Murjiᵓah." He died in 120 AH, but some say 119 AH. It is thus in *Tahdhīb at-tahdhīb*.

Al-Ḥārith ibn ᶜAbdullāh al-Aᶜwar al-Hamdānī the Kūfan who narrated from ᶜAlī, Ibn Masᶜūd and Zayd ibn Thābit, and from whom narrated ash-Shaᶜbī, Abū Isḥāq as-Sabīᶜī, ᶜAṭāᵓ ibn Abī Rabāḥ and a large group. Ash-Shaᶜbī declared him a liar according to what Muslim narrated in the *Muqaddimat aṣ-ṣaḥīḥ*, as did Abū Isḥāq, ᶜAlī ibn al-Madīnī and others. Yaḥyā ibn Maᶜīn declared him to be a trustworthy narrator, and Ibn Ḥibbān said that, "He was in the main a Shīᶜah, who was weak in ḥadīth." He died in 65 AH. Aḥmad ibn Ṣāliḥ al-Miṣrī said, "Al-Ḥārith al-Aᶜwar was a trustworthy narrator. How excellent was his memory and how good is that which he narrates from ᶜAlī!" and he praised him. Someone said to him, "But ash-Shaᶜbī said, 'He used to lie'!" He answered, "He did not lie about ḥadīth but he only used to lie in his personal opinions (*raᵓy*)." Adh-Dhahabī said, "An-Nasāᵓī, along with his stubborn insistence about narrators [that they be impeccable] has used him in proof even though the dominant majority regard him as weak and yet transmit his ḥadīth in the different chapter headings, and this ash-Shaᶜbī calls him a liar and then he later transmits from him! The apparent meaning is that he lies in his citations but not in ḥadīth," as it is in *Tahdhīb at-tahdhīb*.

Al-Ḥārith ibn Abī Dhubāb is al-Ḥārith ibn ʿAbd ar-Raḥmān ibn ʿAbdullāh ibn Saʿd, but some say al-Mughīrah ibn Abī Dhubāb ad-Dawsī the Madīnan. He narrated from his father, his paternal uncle, Saʿīd ibn al-Musayyab, Mujāhid and others. From him narrated Ibn Jurayj, Ismāʿīl inn Umayyah and others. Abū Zurʿah said, "There is no harm in him." Ibn Ḥibbān mentioned him among the trustworthy narrators, and he said, "He was one of those who by the use of skill renders things sound (*mutqin*)." He died in 126 AH. It is thus in *Tahdhīb at-tahdhīb*.

Al-Ḥasan al-Baṣrī is one of the greatest of the Followers and he is al-Ḥasan ibn Abi'l-Ḥasan Yasār. His mother was a mawlāh of Umm Salamah, and he was born two years before the end of the khilāfah of ʿUmar. He moved from Madīnah to Baṣra upon the murder of ʿUthmān. He narrated from a large group of the Companions, and a large group of the Followers narrated from him. He was an imām and a trustworthy narrator, possessing knowledge, doing-without (*zuhd*), scrupulousness (*waraʿ*) and worship. He died in Rajab 110 AH. That is how it is in *Jāmiʿ al-uṣūl*, and there is a very long biography of him in *Tahdhīb at-tahdhīb* and elsewhere.

Al-Ḥasan ibn Muḥammad ibn ʿAlī ibn Abī Ṭālib al-Hāshimī the Madīnan was one of the eminent people of the people of the House (Ahl al-Bayt), and one of the most knowledgeable people on differences of opinion. Al-ʿIjlī regarded him as a trustworthy narrator. Ad-Dāraquṭnī said, "His ḥadīth are ṣaḥīḥ." He died in 95 AH, but some say 101 AH.

Al-Ḥasan ibn ʿUmārah al-Bajalī the Kūfan Abū Muḥammad the qāḍī of Baghdād. He narrated from az-Zuhrī, al-Ḥakam ibn ʿUtaybah, Abū Isḥāq as-Sabīʿī and others, and from him narrated the two Sufyāns and many others. ʿĪsā ibn Yūnus regarded him as a trustworthy narrator, and he said that he was a right-acting shaykh, but many were critical of him as a narrator, among them an-Nasāʾī, Ibn Maʿīn, Ibn al-Madīnī, Aḥmad,

Shu^cbah, ad-Dāraquṭnī, as-Sājī, al-Jūzajānī and others, saying that he is to be abandoned (*matrūk*), or dropped, or he may not be used as a proof, or his ḥadīth are rejected, and the like of that. An-Naḍr said narrated from Shu^cbah, "Al-Ḥasan ibn ^cUmārah transmitted me ḥadīth from al-Ḥakam which had no [genuine] source." He died in 153 AH, as is in *Tahdhīb at-tahdhīb* and elsewhere.

Ḥāṭib ibn Abī Balta^cah ^cAmr ibn ^cUmayr al-Lakhmī the sworn ally of Banī Asad. He was present at Badr, and died in 30 AH, as az-Zurqānī said.

Hazzāl ibn Dhi^ʾāb ibn Yazīd ibn Kulayb al-Aslamī was the one who had a slave girl with whom Mā^ciz had intercourse, and so Hazzāl said to him, "Go to the Messenger of Allah ﷺ and tell him, so that perhaps some Qur^ʾān might be revealed." So he went to him and what happened happened, and so the Prophet ﷺ said to him, "Hazzāl! if only you had veiled him with your robe!" i.e. if only you had not urged him to divulge the secret it would have been better. His son was Nu^caym ibn Hazzāl, and his son Nu^caym ibn Hazzāl about whom said that he was Companion and others said not, and whose son Yazīd was a Follower who was a trustworthy narrator, as Ibn al-Athīr mentioned in *Asad al-ghābah fī ma^crifat aṣ-ṣaḥābah* and *Jāmi^c al-uṣūl.*

Hishām ibn Ismā^cīl ibn Hishām ibn al-Walīd ibn al-Mughīrah al-Makhzūmī. He was governor of Madīnah on behalf of ^cAbd al-Mālik ibn Marwān, and Ibn Ḥibbān mentioned him in the *Kitāb ath-thiqāt.*

Hishām ibn ^cUrwah ibn az-Zubayr ibn al-^cAwwām al-Asadī the Madīnan narrated from his father and his uncle ^cAbdullāh ibn az-Zubayr. From him narrated Mālik, Abū Ḥanīfah and Shu^cbah. Abū Ḥātim and others regarded him as a trustworthy narrator. He died in 145 AH. That is how it is in *Is^cāf al-mubaṭṭa^ʾ* of as-Suyūṭī.

Ḥizām ibn Sa^cīd ibn Muḥayyiṣah is mentioned by Shaykh ^cAbd al-Ḥayy as "Ḥizām ibn Sa^cīd. Thus I have seen it in numerous copies of this book, but what is in *Jāmi*ᶜ *al-uṣūl* by al-Jazarī, the *Taqrīb* of Ibn Ḥajar and the *Is*ᶜ*āf* of as-Suyūṭī was that he was Ḥarām ibn Saᶜd, but some say Ḥarām ibn Sāᶜidah ibn Muḥayyiṣah the Anṣārī and Madīnan Follower who was a trustworthy narrator, but who narrated few ḥadīth. He died in 113 AH in Madīnah.

Ḥudhayfah ibn al-Yamān. Al-Yamān's name was Ḥisl, but it is also said al-Ḥusayl – the diminutive – ibn Jābir ibn ᶜAmr ibn Rabīᶜah al-ᶜAbsī the confederate of Banī ᶜAbd al-Ashhal of the Anṣār. His father was given the honorific nickname of al-Yamān because he spilt some blood among his people and fled to Madīnah where he became a confederate of the Anṣār, and his people called him al-Yamān because he became a confederate of the Anṣār who were from the Yemen. Ḥudhayfah and his father accepted Islam and were both present at Uḥud and al-Yamān was killed in the battle of Uḥud, the Muslims killing him by mistake. Ḥudhayfah gave them [his right to retaliation or compensation for] his blood. Ḥudhayfah was the companion of the secret of the Messenger of Allah ﷺ and has numerous virtues. He died in Madā'in in 36 AH. That is how it is in *Tahdhīb al-asmā' wa'l-lughāt* by an-Nawawī.

Ḥumaydah bint ᶜUbayd ibn Rafāᶜah. Yaḥyā alone among the narrators of the *Muwaṭṭa'* said that she was called Ḥamīdah. Yaḥyā said that she was the daughter of Abū ᶜUbaydah ibn Farwah but that was a mistake of his. The rest of the narrators of the *Muwaṭṭa'* said the daughter of ᶜUbayd ibn Rafāᶜah except for Zayd ibn al-Ḥubāb who said, from Mālik, "The daughter of ᶜUbayd ibn Rāfiᶜ." But the correct position is that [her father was] Rafāᶜah ibn Rāfiᶜ al-Anṣārī as Ibn ᶜAbd al-Barr said. Ibn Mandah took the position that neither she nor her maternal aunt Kabshah were known to have narrated anything other than this ḥadīth, and that thus the single ḥadīth [ḥadīth 90] in the *Muwaṭṭa'* from them was not sound, but al-ᶜAynī said, "Ḥumaydah has another ḥadīth on responding to the person who sneezes which Abū Dāwūd narrated, and a third one narrated by Abū Nu[c]aym. Isḥāq ibn [c]Abdullāh narrated from her and he is a trustworthy narrator."

Ḥumayd ibn [c]Abd ar-Raḥmān was Abū [c]Abd ar-Raḥmān and a Madīnan. Al-[c]Ijlī and others regarded him as a trustworthy narrator. He died in 95 AH, but some say in 105 AH, as is in *Is[c]āf al-mubaṭṭa'* of as-Suyūṭī. Az-Zurqānī said that he was Ḥumayd ibn [c]Abd ar-Raḥmān az-Zuhrī and a Madīnan. He was a trustworthy narrator and one of the major Followers. Yaḥyā ibn Yaḥyā al-Laythī added in his transmission of the *Muwaṭṭa'* that he was the son of [c]Abd ar-Raḥmān ibn [c]Awf.

Ḥumayd ibn Mālik ibn al-Khaytham. This is how we found it expressed in some copies upon which the commentary of al-Qārī is based and he spelt al-Khaytham thus. Ibn Ḥajar in *at-Taqrīb* spelt it as a diminutive when he said, "Ḥumayd ibn Mālik ibn Khuthaym, and it is said that Mālik was his grandfather and the name of his father was [c]Abdullāh. He was a trustworthy narrator." He mentioned in *Tahdhīb at-tahdhīb* about its spelling something different when he said in his biographical notice about him, "Ibn Sa[c]d said, 'He was from the old generation and had few ḥadīth.' Ibn Ḥibbān mentioned him in *ath-Thiqāt,* and al-Bukhārī mentioned his grandfather in *at-Tārīkh* where he spelled him among those who narrated from him as al-Khutam. In the narration of Ibn al-Qāsim of al-*Muwaṭṭa'* they spelt it like that but with a 'tha' as Khutham, and Muslim spelt it like that but as al-Khuttam. They spelt it in *al-Aḥkām* by Ismā[c]īl al-Qadi as al-Khuththam." (Abridged) Ibn al-Athīr spelt it in *an-Nihāyah* as it is spelt in *at-Taqrīb.*

Ḥumayd ibn Qays was Abū Ṣafwān al-A[c]raj al-Qārī'. There was no harm in him, and he was one of the narrators of whom everybody availed. He died in 130 AH, but some say after that, as az-Zurqānī mentioned.

Ḥumayd aṭ-Ṭawīl was Ḥumayd ibn Abī Ḥumayd Abū [c]Ubaydah the Baṣran aṭ-Ṭawīl. He narrated from Anas, al-Ḥasan and [c]Ikrimah, and from him narrated Mālik, Shu[c]bah, the two Ḥammāds, the two Sufyāns and many others. Ibn Ma[c]īn and Abū Ḥātim declared him to be a trustworthy narrator. He died in 143 AH as is in *Isᶜāf al-mubaṭṭaʾ* of as-Suyūṭī.

Al-Ḥuraqah are a tribe from Hamdān, Ibn Ḥibbān said, or from Juhaynah as ad-Dāraquṭnī said and that is the sound position. That is how it is in *Ansāb as-Samᶜānī*.

Ḥuṣayn ibn ᶜAbd ar-Raḥmān as-Sulamī the Kūfan Abu'l-Hudhayl son of the paternal uncle of Manṣūr ibn al-Muᶜtamir. He narrated from Jābir ibn Samurah, ᶜAmārah ibn Ruwaybah, Ibn Abī Laylā and Abū Wāʾil. From him narrated Shuᶜbah, Abū ᶜAwānah and others. He was a trustworthy narrator and a decisive proof and a ḥāfiẓ with short chains of transmission. Aḥmad said, "Ḥuṣayn is a trustworthy narrator who is to be trusted, and he is one of the great ones of the people of ḥadīth." He lived for 93 years and died in 136 AH. That is how it is in *Tadhkirat al-ḥuffāẓ*.

Ḥuṣayn ibn Ibrāhīm [ḥadīth 263]. That is how it is in the present copy, and I have not come across his condition in *Tahdhīb at-tahdhīb, Taqrīb at-tahdhīb, al-Kāshif, Jāmiᶜ al-uṣūl, Mīzān al-iᶜtidāl* and others. Previously I came across in my research into the subject of raising the hands [in prayer] a narration from Abū Yūsuf Yaᶜqūb ibn Ibrāhīm from Ḥuṣayn ibn ᶜAbd ar-Raḥmān, where it transpired that he was one of his higher shaykhs, and so perhaps it is him. In the book *al-Ḥujjaj* it is: Ḥuṣayn from Ibrāhīm so it seems that specifically al-Ḥuṣayn is the former and Ibrāhīm is an-Nakhaᶜī.

Ḥuṣayn ibn Miḥṣan. Ibn Ḥibbān mentions him in *Thiqāt at-tābiᶜīn*. Ibn as-Sakan said, "It is said that he was a Companions except that his narration is from his paternal aunt and he has no narrations from the Messenger of Allah ﷺ," as is in *Tahdhīb at-tahdhīb* and *Taqrīb at-tahdhīb*.

I

Ibn ᶜAbbās is ᶜAbdullāh ibn ᶜAbbās ibn ᶜAbd al-Muṭṭalib al-Hāshimī, the son of the paternal uncle of the Messenger of Allah ﷺ who is known as the Learned Man and the Ocean because of the great amount of his knowledge. He has very famous merits which are mentioned in the books about the Companions such as *Asad al-ghābah*, the *al-Iṣābah* and others. He died in Ṭāʾif in 68 AH, but some say 69 AH, and others 70 AH. That is mentioned in *at-Tahdhīb*. Al-ᶜAynī said in *al-Bināyah sharḥ al-Hidāyah* in the book on the Ḥajj concerning the investigation on the stopping at Muzdalifah, "When one uses 'Ibn ᶜAbbās' unqualifiedly one only means ᶜAbdullāh ibn ᶜAbbās." He also mentioned in *al-Bināyah* in the book *al-Ḥazr wa'l-ibāḥah* that ḥadīth scholars use as their technical terms when they mention ᶜAbdullāh that they mean ᶜAbdullāh ibn Masᶜūd even if others are included apparently [in that designation]. Similarly they say Ibn ᶜUmar meaning ᶜAbdullāh ibn ᶜUmar even though ᶜUmar had other sons apart from ᶜAbdullāh." ᶜAlī al-Qārī the Makkan said in *Jamᶜ al-wasāʾil bi sharḥ ash-shamāʾil*, i.e. [the commentary on] the *Shamāʾil* of at-Tirmidhī, "The technical usage of ḥadīth scholars is that if ᶜAlī is used unqualifiedly at the end of the [list of] names [in an isnād] then it is ᶜAlī ibn Abī Ṭālib, and that if ᶜAbdullāh is used unqualifiedly then it is ᶜAbdullāh ibn Masᶜūd, and that where al-Ḥasan is used without qualification it is al-Ḥasan al-Baṣrī. It is similar with the unqualified use of Abū Bakr, ᶜUmar and ᶜUthmān." Al-Qārī also said in his book *al-Athmār al-janiyyah fī ṭabaqāt al-ḥanafiyyah*, "When Ibn ᶜAbbās is used unqualifiedly only ᶜAbdullāh is meant. It is similarly when Ibn ᶜUmar and Ibn az-Zubayr are used without qualification. As for when ᶜAbdullāh is used without qualification then it is ᶜAbdullāh ibn Masᶜūd in the technical usage of the people of knowledge among the fuqahāʾ and the scholars of ḥadīth." This ought to be memorised because it is useful.

Ibn ᶜAbd ar-Raḥmān ibn Abī Hurayrah [ḥadīth 648]. See ᶜAbd ar-Raḥmān ibn Abī Hurayrah.

Ibn Abī Aḥmad was ᶜAbdullāh ibn Abī Aḥmad Jahsh of Quraysh al-Asadī. A large number mention him as one of the trustworthy narrators of the Followers. That is what az-Zurqānī said.

Ibn Abī Dhi'b is Muḥammad ibn ᶜAbd ar-Raḥmān ibn al-Mughīrah ibn Abī Dhi'b the Madīnan who narrated from ᶜIkrimah, Nāfiᶜ and a large number of others, and from whom narrated Muᶜammar, Ibn al-Mubārak and Yaḥyā al-Qaṭṭān, as adh-Dhahabī mentioned in *al-Kāshif.*

Ibn Abī Mulaykah is ᶜAbdullāh ibn ᶜUbaydullāh ibn ᶜAbdullāh ibn Abī Mulaykah whose name was Zuhayr at-Taymī. He was a trustworthy narrator and a faqīh. He died in 117 AH, as az-Zurqānī said.

Ibn Abī Qatādah was ᶜAbdullāh ibn Abī Qatādah the Madīnan and he was a trustworthy narrator and one of the Followers. He died in 95 AH. Ibn Saᶜd said, "Thābit ibn Abī Qatādah married her [Kabshah] and she bore him children." In the narration of Ibn al-Mubārak there is that Mālik said she [Kabshah] was the wife of Abū Qatādah but Ibn ᶜAbd al-Barr said that this was his mistake and that she was married to his son. Az-Zurqānī said so.

Ibn Buḥaynah from the name of his mother by which [kunyā] he became known. He is ᶜAbdullāh ibn Mālik ibn al-Qashab al-Azdī and is one of the great ones of the Companions. He died after 50 AH. That is how it is in *at-Taqrīb* and elsewhere.

Ibn Jurayj is ᶜAbd al-Mālik ibn ᶜAbd al-ᶜAzīz Ibn Jurayj al-Umawī, their mawlā, the Makkan the faqīh. He was an eminent trustworthy narrator. He died in 150 AH or after. That is how it is in *at-Taqrīb* and *al-Kāshif.*

Ibn Masᶜūd. See ᶜAbdullāh ibn Masᶜūd.

Ibn Mirs. It is spelt thus in *al-Mughnī*and he said, "He was a mawlā of Qurasyh."

Ibn Muᶜammar ibn ᶜUthmān ibn ᶜAmr ibn Saᶜd ibn Taym of Quraysh was one of the notables of Quraysh and one of their nobles. He died in

Damascus in 82 AH. His grandfather was Muᶜammar the Companion, the son of the paternal uncle of Abū Quḥāfah the father of Abū Bakr aṣ-Ṣiddīq, az-Zurqānī said.

Ibn Shihāb az-Zuhrī. Az-Zuhri denotes his relationship to Zuhrah ibn Kilāb ibn Murrah ibn Kaᶜb ibn Luʾayy. That is how it is in *al-Ansāb*. An-Nawawī said in *Tahdhīb al-asmāʾ wa'l-lughāt*: "Muḥammad ibn Muslim ibn ᶜUbaydullāh ibn ᶜAbdullāh Ibn Shihāb ibn ᶜAbdullāh ibn al-Ḥārith ibn Zuhrah ibn Kilāb ibn Murrah ibn Kaᶜb ibn Luʾayy Abū Bakr of Quraysh az-Zuhrī the Madīnan. He lived in Shām and was at Aylah. Sometimes they say, "az-Zuhrī" and sometimes "Ibn Shihāb" ascribing him to his grandfather's grandfather. He was a minor Follower [in that he didn't meet as many of the Companions as major Followers had], and he heard from Anas, Sahl ibn Saᶜd, as-Sāʾib ibn Yazīd, Abū Umāmah and Abu'ṭ-Ṭufayl. A great number of the major Followers and their Followers narrated from him. We narrate that al-Layth ibn Saᶜd said, 'I have never seen an ᶜālim more comprehensive than Ibn Shihāb, nor one who was more knowledgeable than him.' Ash-Shāfiᶜī said, 'If it had not been for az-Zuhrī the Sunnahs would have left Madīnah.' He died in Ramaḍān of 124 AH, and was buried in a town on the outskirts of Shām called Shaghab." (Abridged)

Ibn Sīrīn. His name was Muḥammad. An-Nawawī mentioned in *at-Tahdhīb* that his father – Sīrīn – was the mawlā of Anas ibn Mālik, and that he had six children: Muḥammad, Maᶜbad, Anas, Yaḥyā, Ḥafṣah and Karīmah, all of whom are trustworthy narrators and among the eminent Followers. Most often when Ibn Sīrīn is used unqualifiedly it refers to this Muḥammad Abū Bakr the Baṣran and imām in tafsīr, interpretation of dreams, ḥadīth and fiqh. He heard from Ibn ᶜUmar, Abū Hurayrah, Ibn az-Zubayr and others, but he did not hear from Ibn ᶜAbbās, so that his ḥadīth from him are mursal. The imāms praised him a great deal. He died in Baṣra in 110 AH.

Ibn Suhayl ibn Abī Ṣāliḥ. See Suhayl ibn Abī Ṣāliḥ.

Ibn Ukaymah [the diminutive of Akmah]. His name was ᶜUmārah but it is also said it was ᶜAmmār and some say ᶜAmr and some say ᶜĀmir al-Laythī Abu'l-Walīd the Madīnan. He was a trustworthy narrator and died in 101 AH. That was what az-Zurqānī said.

Ibn Umm Maktūm's name was ᶜAmr, but some say Ḥuṣayn. The Prophet ﷺ named him ᶜAbdullāh. He accepted Islam of old and was present at the battle of Qādisiyyah [15 AH/636 CE] in the khilāfah of ᶜUmar where he was shahīd. The best known thing about his father's name is that he was Qays ibn Zāʾidah, and that his mother's name was ᶜĀtikah from Makhzūm. One of them claimed that he was born blind and that his mother was given her kunyā because of him [Umm Maktūm – mother of the blind one] because of the concealing of the light of his sight, as az-Zurqānī mentioned.

Ibn az-Zubayr [ḥadīth 118] see Abu'z-Zubayr.

Ibrāhīm ibn ᶜAbdullāh ibn Hunay al-Hāshimī – he was their mawlā – was a Follower who was Madīnan. Ibn Saᶜd said, "He was a trustworthy narrator who narrated a great many ḥadīth and from whom all narrated." He died after the first century as az-Zurqānī mentioned.

Ibrāhīm ibn Muḥammad is Ibrāhīm ibn Muḥammad ibn Abī Yaḥyā whose name is Samᶜān al-Aslamī Abū Isḥāq the Madīnan about whom there is disagreement as to whether he is trustworthy or weak. He said in *Tahdhīb al-kamāl* and *Tahdhīb at-tahdhīb*, "He narrated from az-Zuhrī, Yaḥyā ibn Saᶜīd al-Anṣārī, Ṣāliḥ the mawlā of at-Tawʾamah (the twin), Muḥammad ibn al-Munkadir and others. From him narrated ath-Thawrī, ash-Shāfiᶜī, and Abū Nuᶜaym. Abū Ṭālib said narrating from Aḥmad, 'His ḥadīth are not to be written. He used to narrate rejected ḥadīth without any source.' Ash-Shāfiᶜī said, 'Trustworthy in ḥadīth.' Ibn ᶜAdī said, 'I asked Aḥmad ibn Muḥammad ibn Saᶜīd,' – meaing Ibn ᶜAqdah – '"Do you know anyone who spoke well about Ibrāhīm other than ash-Shāfiᶜī?" He said, "Yes. Aḥmad ibn Yaḥyā narrated to us, 'I heard Hamdān ibn al-Aṣbahānī. I asked, "Do you base your dīn on the ḥadīth of Ibrāhīm?"

He said, "Yes."'" Then Aḥmad ibn Muḥammad ibn Saᶜīd said to me, "I examined the ḥadīth of Ibrāhīm a great deal and he is not someone whose ḥadīth are rejected."' Ibn ᶜAdī said, 'And this is what he said as he said it. And I have also examined his ḥadīth a great deal and I do not find among them any which are rejected except from shaykhs who interpret and he is among those whose ḥadīth are to be recorded. He has a *Muwaṭṭa*ʾ which is a number of sizes larger than the *Muwaṭṭa*ʾ of Mālik. He died in 184 AH, but some say 191 AH.'"

Ibrāhīm ibn ᶜUqbah. He said in *al-Isᶜāf*, "Aḥmad, Yaḥyā and an-Nasāʾī regarded him as a trustworthy narrator." ᶜUqbah was Madīnan.

Ibrāhīm ibn Yazīd al-Umawī al-Khūzī the Makkan and mawlā of ᶜUmar ibn ᶜAbd al-ᶜAzīz. He narrated from Ṭāwūs, ᶜAṭāʾ, Abu'z-Zubayr and others, and from him narrated Wakīᶜ, ᶜAbd ar-Razzāq, and ath-Thawrī. Ibn Maᶜīn said, "He is not a trustworthy narrator, and he is nothing." Abū Zurᶜah, Abū Ḥātim and Ibn Numayr regarded him as weak. Abū Zurᶜah and Abū Ḥātim said, "His ḥadīth are rejected." Al-Bukhārī said, "They were silent [in narrating] from him," and ad-Dūlābī said, "meaning that they abandoned him." An-Nasāʾī said, "Abandoned." Ibn ᶜAdī said, "He is numbered among those whose ḥadīth are written down even if he is considered weak." He died in 151 AH, as is in *Tahdhīb al-kamāl*.

Ibrāhīm an-Nakhaᶜī is by ascription to Nakhaᶜ a tribe of the Arabs which settled in Kūfa from where their fame spread. Ibn Mākūlā said, "From this tribe are ᶜAlqamah, al-Aswad and Ibrāhīm. That is how it is in the *Ansāb* of as-Samᶜānī." He mentioned in *Tahdhīb at-tahdhīb*, "Ibrāhīm ibn Yazīd ibn Qays ibn al-Aswad ibn ᶜAmr Abū ᶜImrān an-Nakhaᶜī the Kūfan, the muftī of the people of Kūfa was right-acting man and a faqīh." Al-Aᶜmash said, "He was good in ḥadīth." Ash-Shaᶜbī said, "He left after him no one more knowledgeable than himself." Abū Saᶜīd al-ᶜAlāʾī said, "He very often used mursal ḥadīth [which he ascribed directly to the Prophet ﷺ without mentioning the Companion or Companions from whom he heard them] and a body of the imāms regard his mursal ḥadīth as sound." Al-Aᶜmash said, "I said to Ibrāhīm, 'Give me something from Ibn Masᶜūd with a chain of transmission.' He said, 'If I narrate you something from a man from ᶜAbdullāh that is what I heard. If I say, "ᶜAbdullāh said…" then it is from more than one person.'" Abū Ḥātim said, "an-Nakhaᶜī did not meet any of the Companions except for ᶜĀ'ishah, but he did not hear anything from her, and he reached Anas but he did not hear anything from him." He was born in 55 AH and died in 96 AH.

An informant [ḥadīth 880]. In the *Muwaṭṭa'* of Yaḥyā it is that, "…Mālik that it had reached him that ᶜUmar …" Its commentator said, "Those things about which Mālik said they 'reached' him are ṣaḥīḥ, as Ibn ᶜUyaynah said."

ᶜIrāk ibn Mālik. As-Suyūṭī said in *Isᶜāf al-mubaṭṭa'*, "ᶜIrāk ibn Mālik al-Ghifārī, by ascription to the tribe of Banī Ghifār, the Madīnan narrated from Ibn ᶜAbbās, Abū Hurayrah, Ibn ᶜUmar, ᶜĀ'ishah and a large group of people, and from him narrated Sulaymān ibn Yasār, Khaytham and ᶜAbdullāh the two sons of ᶜIrāk. Abū Zurᶜah and Abū Ḥātim regarded him as a trustworthy narrator. He died in Madīnah in the khilāfah of Yazīd ibn ᶜAbd al-Mālik." This spelling – ᶜIrāk – is what Ibn Ḥajar used in *at-Taqrīb*, Ibn al-Athīr in *Jāmiᶜ al-uṣūl*, and al-Fattanī in *al-Mughnī* and others.

ᶜĪsā ibn Abī ᶜĪsā al-Khayyāṭ al-Madīnī. Adh-Dhahabī said in *al-Kāshif*, "ᶜĪsā ibn Abī ᶜĪsā al-Khayyāṭ narrated from his father and from ash-Shaᶜbī and a number of others, and from him narrated Wakīᶜ, Ibn Abī Fudayk and a number of others. They declared him weak. He is a Kūfan who resided in Madīnah. He was a tailor and then seller of wheat. He died in 151 AH." There is in *at-Taqrīb*, "ᶜĪsā ibn Abī ᶜĪsā al-Ḥannāṭ al-Ghifārī Abū Mūsā al-Madīnī whose origin was in Kūfa. His father's name was Maysarah. He is called al-Khayyāṭ – the tailor – and al-Ḥannāṭ – the seller of wheat – and he had dealt with the three trades [the third was selling a type of leaf as camel fodder]. He is abandoned [as a narrator], of the sixth generation. He died in 51 AH, but some say before that."

ᶜĪsā ibn Ṭalḥah ibn ᶜUbaydullāh was an eminent trustworthy narrator. He died in 100 AH, and his father was one of the Ten [promised the Garden], as al-Ḥāfiẓ said.

Isḥāq ibn ᶜAbdullāh ibn Abī Ṭalḥah. As-Suyūṭī said, "Abū Zurᶜah, Abū Ḥātim and an-Nasāʾī regarded him as trustworthy. Ibn Maᶜīn said, "Trustworthy and a decisive argument." He died in 134 AH. [His grandfather Abū Ṭalḥah] was Zayd ibn Sahl.

Isḥāq ibn Rāshid was Abū Sulaymān Isḥāq ibn Rāshid al-Ḥarrānī, but some say ar-Raqī , the mawlā of Banī Umayyah, but some say the mawlā of ᶜUmar. He narrated from az-Zuhrī, ᶜAbdullāh ibn Ḥasan ibn al-Ḥasan ibn ᶜAlī, Muḥammad ibn ᶜAlī Zayn al-ᶜĀbidīn Abū Jaᶜfar al-Bāqir and others, and from him narrated a whole group. Ibn Ḥibbān and Ibn Shahīn mentioned him among the trustworthy narrators, and an-Nasāʾī, Ibn Maᶜīn and Abū Ḥātim regarded him as a trustworthy narrator, as is in *Tahdhīb at-tahdhīb* and other books.

Ismāᶜīl ibn Abī Khālid al-Aḥmasī, their mawlā, the Kūfan, by ascription to al-Aḥmas a party of Bajlah who resided in Kūfa, as as-Samᶜānī mentioned. He narrated from his father, Abū Juḥayfah, ᶜAbdullāh ibn Abī Awfā, Qays ibn Abī Ḥāzim – from whom he narrated a great deal – and others. From him narrated Shuᶜbah, the two Sufyāns, Ibn al-Mubārak, Yaḥyā al-Qaṭṭān and others. Ibn Maᶜīn, Ibn Mahdī and an-Nasāʾī said that he was a trustworthy narrator. Al-ᶜIjlī said, "A trustworthy Kūfan Follower." Abū Ḥātim said, "I do not give precedence over him to any other of ash-Shaᶜbī's companions, and he is a trustworthy narrator. He died in 126 AH." Thus it is in *Tahdhīb at-tahdhīb*.

Ismāᶜīl ibn ᶜAyyāsh al-ᶜAnbasī Abū ᶜUtbah al-Ḥimṣī. Yaᶜqūb ibn Sufyān said, "Some people spoke about him [negatively] but he is a trustworthy narrator, a just man, the most knowledgeable of people of the ḥadīth of the people of Shām. The most that they said was he narrated unusual things [perhaps in the sense of unusual ḥadīth (*gharā᾽ib*) having a single narrator at some stage of the chain of transmission] from the trustworthy narrators of Madīnah and Makkah." Yazīd ibn Hārūn said, "I have not seen anyone who memorised more than Ismāᶜīl ibn ᶜAyyāsh, I do not know, perhaps not even Sufyān ath-Thawrī." ᶜUthmān ad-Dārimī said, "I hope that there should be no harm in him." Muḥammad ibn ᶜUthmān ibn Abī Shaybah narrated from Yaḥyā ibn Maᶜīn, "A trustworthy narrator in that which he narrates from the people of Shām. As for his narrations from the people of Ḥijāz, his book was lost and he became mixed up in his memorisation from them. He died in 181 AH, but some say 182 AH." It is thus in *Tahdhīb at-tahdhīb*.

Ismāᶜīl ibn Ḥakīm [ḥadīth 873] was Ismāᶜīl ibn Abī Ḥakīm of Quraysh. Ibn Maᶜīn and an-Nasā᾽ī regarded him as a trustworthy narrator. He died in 130 AH, as az-Zurqānī mentioned.

Ismāᶜīl ibn Ibrāhīm [ḥadīth 263]. In *Tahdhīb at-tahdhīb* and *al-Mīzān*, he mentioned many with this name and lineage some of whom were trustworthy narrators and some of whom were weak. Apparently the person mentioned here is Ismāᶜīl ibn Ibrāhīm ibn Muhājir al-Bajalī and an-Nakhaᶜī the Kūfan whom al-Bukhārī and an-Nasā᾽ī regarded as weak. Abū Ḥātim said, "He is not strong, but his ḥadīth are to be written. He narrated from his father, Ismāᶜīl ibn Abī Khālid and others, and from him narrated Ibn Numayr, Wakīᶜ, Ṭalq ibn Ghanām, Abū ᶜAlī al-Ḥanafī and others."

Ismāᶜīl ibn Ibrāhīm ibn Muqsim al-Asadī – their mawlā – Abū Bishr the Baṣran who is best known as Ibn ᶜUlayyah a dimunitive from his mother's name, but some say his maternal grandmother. He used to dislike being called that to such an extent that he used to say, "Whoever calls me that is backbiting me." He narrated from ᶜAbd al-ᶜAzīz ibn Suhayb, Ḥumayd aṭ-Ṭawīl, Ayyūb, Ibn ᶜAwn and others. From him narrated Shuᶜbah, Ibn Jurayj and others. Ibn Saᶜd, an-Nasā᾽ī and others declared him to be a trustworthy narrator. He died in 193 AH. He has a long biographical notice comprising high praise in *Tahdhīb at-tahdhīb* and elsewhere.

Ismāᶜīl ibn Muḥammad ibn Saᶜd Abū Muḥammad the Madīnan is trustworthy and a decisive proof and one of the Followers. He died in 134 AH. He was the grandson of Saᶜd ibn Abī Waqqāṣ. The five narrated from him. Thus it is in *Taqrīb at-tahdhīb*.

Ismāᶜīl ibn Muḥammad ibn Thābit ibn Qays ibn Shammās al-Anṣārī the Madīnan. Ibn Ḥibbān mentioned him in *Thiqat at-Tabi'in*.

Isrāʾīl ibn Yūnus is Abū Yūsuf Isrāʾīl ibn Yūnus ibn Abī Isḥāq as-Sabīᶜī al-Hamdānī the Kūfan. He narrated from his grandfather whom we have mentioned before, Ziyād ibn ᶜAlāqah, ᶜĀṣim al-Aḥwāl and others. From him narrated ᶜAbd ar-Razzāq, Wakīᶜ and a large group. Aḥmad said, "He was a shaykh who was a trustworthy narrator." Abū Ḥātim said, "A trustworthy narrator who was utterly truthful." Al-ᶜIjlī regarded him as a trustworthy narrator as did Yaᶜqūb ibn Shaybah, Abū Dāwūd, an-Nasāʾī and others. He died in 162 AH or 165 AH or 161 AH according to the different sayings. That is how it is in *Tahdhīb at-tahdhīb*.

J

Jābir ibn ᶜAbdullāh, Abū ᶜAbdullāh but some say Abū ᶜAbd ar-Raḥmān and even Abū Muḥammad. He went on expeditions with the Prophet ﷺ nineteen times but he was not present at Badr. He died in Madīnah, but some say Makkah, in 78 AH, and others say 79 AH and even 74 AH. That is how it is in *Isᶜāf al-mubaṭṭa'* of as-Suyūṭī. Jābir is Abū ᶜAbdullāh Jābir ibn ᶜAbdullāh ibn ᶜAmr ibn Ḥarām ibn ᶜAmr ibn Sawād ibn Salamah al-Anṣārī one of the most famous of the Companions. He was present at Badr – according to what is said – and what came after it. His father was one of the twelve leading men [to pledge allegiance at al-ᶜAqabah]. Jābir became blind at the end of his life, and he died in Madīnah in 74 AH, but some say 77 or 78 AH, and he was the last of the Companions to die in Madīnah. Thus it is in *Jāmiᶜ al-uṣūl*.

Jābir ibn ᶜAbdullāh al-Ḥarāmī – by ascription to Ḥarām ibn Kaᶜb al-Anṣārī [ḥadīth 454]. He was the grandfather[5] of Jābir ibn ᶜAbdullāh, as as-Samᶜānī mentioned.

Jābir ibn ᶜAtīk was a major Companion. He died in 61 AH, as az-Zurqānī mentioned.

Jābir al-Juᶜfī is someone about whom there is discussion, and even if some critics regard him as a trustworthy narrator, the dominant majority – among them Abū Ḥanīfah – criticise him strongly and abandon him. As-Samᶜānī mentions in *al-Ansāb* after mentioning that, "Al-Juᶜfī (by ascription to a tribe of Kūfa, Juᶜfī ibn Saᶜd of Mudhḥij) is Abū Yazīd Jābir al-Juᶜfī one of the people of Kūfa who narrates from ᶜAṭā' and ash-Shaᶜbī, and from whom narrates ath-Thawrī and Shuᶜbah. He died in 128 AH and he was a Sabaite and one of the companions of ᶜAbdullāh ibn Saba'.[6]

[5] If he was the grandfather, then he must have been the maternal grandfather, because his paternal grandfather was ᶜAmr ibn Ḥarām ibn ᶜAmr. The *Muwaṭṭa'* of Yaḥyā has simply Jābir ibn ᶜAbdullāh. He himself could have been named al-Ḥarāmī because of his great grandfather, and Allah knows best.

[6] ᶜAbdullāh ibn Saba' was a notorious extreme shīᶜah from a jewish background.

He used to say, '"Alī ﷺ will return to the world.' Yaḥyā ibn Maᶜīn said, 'He was a liar who believed in returning to the present state of existence after death.'" He mentioned in *Tahdhīb at-tahdhīb,* "Jābir ibn Yazīd ibn al-Ḥārith Abū ᶜAbdullāh al-Juᶜfī is said to be Abū Yazīd the Kūfan. He narrated from Abu'ṭ-Ṭufayl, Abu'ḍ-Ḍuḥā, ᶜIkrimah, ᶜAṭāʾ, Ṭāwūs and a large group. From him narrated Shuᶜbah, ath-Thawrī, Isrāʾīl, al-Ḥasan ibn Ḥayy, Sharīk, Misᶜar and others. Ibn ᶜUlayyah said [narrating] from Shuᶜbah, 'Jābir was utterly truthful in ḥadīth.' Wakīᶜ said, 'Whatever you are in doubt about, do not doubt that Jābir was a trustworthy narrator.' Ath-Thawri said to Shuᶜbah, 'If you talk disparagingly about Jābir, I will talk about you.' Ibn Maᶜīn said, 'He was a liar.' Once he said, 'His ḥadīth are not to be written.' Yaḥyā ibn Saᶜīd said [narrating] from Ismāᶜīl ibn Abī Khālid that ash-Shaᶜbī said to Jābir, 'You will not die until you have lied against the Messenger of Allah ﷺ.' Ismāᶜīl said, 'Days and nights had not passed before he was suspected of lying.' Someone said to Zāʾidah, 'Why do you not narrate from Ibn Abī Laylā, Jābir al-Juᶜfī and al-Kalbī?' He said, 'As for al-Juᶜfī, by Allah! he was a liar who believed in returning to this existence after death.' Abū Yaḥyā al-Ḥimmānī said [narrating from Abū Ḥanīfah, 'I have never met among those I have met anyone more given to lying than al-Juᶜfī. I never brought him any of my views but that he brought me a tradition about it claiming that he had thirty thousand ḥadīth which he had not made public.' Aḥmad said, 'Yaḥyā al-Qaṭṭān and ᶜAbd ar-Raḥmān ibn Mahdī abandoned him.' An-Nasāʾī said, 'His ḥadīth are abandoned,' and he once said, 'He is not a trustworthy narrator; his ḥadīth are not to be written.' Al-Ḥākim said, 'His ḥadīth are gone.' Ibn ᶜAdī said, 'He has good ḥadīth, but he is closer to being weak than to being truthful.' Ayyūb, Layth ibn Abī Sālim and al-Jūzajānī said he was a liar, and similarly Ibn ᶜUyaynah, Aḥmad and Saᶜīd ibn Jubayr." (Abridged)

Ja^{c}far ibn Muḥammad is the Imām Abū ^{c}Abdullāh Ja^{c}far aṣ-Ṣādiq al-Hāshimī, Madīnan, ibn Muḥammad – who was well known as al-Bāqir – ibn ^{c}Alī – who was well known as Zayn al-^{c}Ābidīn – ibn Ḥusayn ibn ^{c}Alī ibn Abī Ṭālib. He was one of the chiefs of the Ahl al-Bayt and one of the devoted worshippers of the Followers of the Followers. He was born in 80 AH in Madīnah and died there in 148 AH. He narrated from his father and from ^{c}Aṭāʾ, ^{c}Urwah and a large group of people, and from him narrated Mālik, Abū Ḥanīfah, Yaḥyā ibn Sa^{c}īd al-Anṣārī, Shu^{c}bah, the two Sufyāns and others. Ibn Ma^{c}īn said that he was a trusted and trustworthy narrator. Abū Ḥātim said, "He was a trustworthy narrator, the like of whom is not to be asked about," as is in *Is^{c}āf al-mubaṭṭaʾ* of as-Suyūṭī. His father was Muḥammad al-Bāqir.

Jamīl al-Muʾadhdhin was Jamīl ibn ^{c}Abd ar-Raḥmān al-Mu'adhdhin the Madīnan. His mother was one of the children of Sa^{c}d al-Qarẓ. He heard from Sa^{c}īd ibn al-Musayyab and ^{c}Umar ibn ^{c}Abd al-^{c}Azīz, and Mālik narrated from him through Yaḥyā ibn Sa^{c}īd and directly without intermediary, as az-Zurqānī said.

Jarīr ibn ^{c}Uthmān. As-Sam^{c}ānī mentioned him in *al-Ansāb* in relation to ar-Raḥabī – by ascription to Raḥabah a clan of Ḥimyar, and he said, "One of those related to him is Abū ^{c}Uthmān Jarīr ibn ^{c}Uthmān ibn Jabr ibn Aḥmar ibn As^{c}ad ar-Raḥabī al-Ḥimṣī, he is called Abū ^{c}Awn. He listened to ^{c}Abdullāh ibn Busr the Companion, Rashīd ibn Sa^{c}d, ^{c}Abd ar-Raḥmān ibn Maysarah and others. From him narrated Baqiyyah, Ismā^{c}īl ibn ^{c}Ayyāsh, ^{c}Īsā ibn Yūnus, Mu^{c}ādh ibn Mu^{c}ādh al-^{c}Anbarī, al-Ḥakam ibn Nāfi^c and a large group apart from them. He was a reliable trustworthy narrator. Al-^{c}Ijlī said, 'Jarīr from Shām is a trustworthy narrator. It is quoted of him that he used to abuse ^{c}Alī ibn Abī Ṭālib, and it is also quoted of him that he returned from that position. He was born in 80 AH, and died in 163 AH.'" (Abridged)

J

Al-Jarrāḥ the mawlā of Umm Ḥabībah. As-Suyūṭī said in *Isʿāf al-mubaṭṭaʾ* that his honorific was Abu'l-Jarrāḥ. He narrated from his former owner Umm Ḥabībah. ʿUthmān, and Sālim and others narrated from him. Ibn Ḥibbān declared him a trustworthy narrator. It is also said that his name was az-Zubayr.

Jubayr ibn Muṭʿim ibn ʿAdī ibn Nawfal ibn ʿAbd Manāf was a Companion who accepted Islam on the day of the Opening [of Makkah to Islam]. He died in 58 AH or 59 AH, as az-Zurqānī mentioned.

Jumhān the mawlā of the tribe of Aslam [ḥadīth 562]. He was a Madīnan of the old generation and acceptable, as Ibn Ḥajar said in *Taqrīb at-tahdhīb.* In *Tahdhīb at-tahdhīb* there is that he was Jumhān Abu'l-ʿAlāʾ, but some say Abū Yaʿlā, the mawlā of the tribe of Aslam, who is counted as one of the Madīnans. He narrated from ʿUthmān, Saʿd, Abū Hurayrah, Umm Bakrah al-Aslamiyyah. From him narrated ʿUrwah, ʿUmar ibn Nabīh. Muslim mentioned him in the first generation of the people of Madīnah, and Ibn Ḥibbān mentioned him in *ath-Thiqāt*. ʿAlī ibn al-Madīnī said, "He was my mother's grandfather, who was one of those taken prisoner as far as I know." (Abridged.) Al-Qārī mistakenly spelt his name Jamhān.

K

Kaᶜb al-Aḥbār. See Kaᶜb ibn Qāniᶜ.

Kaᶜb ibn Qāniᶜ Abū Isḥāq al-Ḥimyarī is one of the great Followers, better known as Kaᶜb al-Aḥbār who was one of the Muslims from the People of the Book. Muᶜāwiyah said, "He is the most truthful of these who narrate from the Book." He died in 32 AH in Ḥimṣ, as is in *Isᶜāf al-mubaṭṭaʾ* of as-Suyūṭī.

Kaᶜb ibn ᶜUjrah ibn Umayyah ibn ᶜAdī al-Anṣārī who went to reside in Kūfa and who died in Madāʾin 51 AH or later. Ibn ᶜUmar, Ibn ᶜAbbās and others narrated from him and of the Followers, Ibn Abī Laylā, Abū Wāʾil and others. Ibn al-Athīr said, "He was with the Messenger of Allah ﷺ at al-Ḥudaybiyyah in iḥrām, and the Messenger of Allah ﷺ saw him with lice falling from his head on to his face, and so he asked him, "Do your vermin bother you?" He answered, "Yes." So he told him to shave [his head], and Allah revealed about it his saying, "If any of you are ill or have a head injury," (Sūrat al-Baqarah: 195) meaning "do not shave your heads in the state of iḥrām unless you are compelled to do so by a sickness or an affliction of the head such as vermin or a headache."

Kabshah bint Kaᶜb ibn Mālik al-Anṣārīyyah the wife of Ibn Abī Qatādah and the maternal aunt of Ḥumaydah. It is said that she was a Companion. Ibn Ḥibbān regarded her as a trustworthy narrator and said she was a Companion.

Kathīr ibn aṣ-Ṣalt al-Kindī was a major Madīnan Follower, who was born during the lifetime of the Messenger of Allah ﷺ. Those who regard him as a Companion make a mistake, as az-Zurqānī said.

Kaysān ibn Saᶜīd al-Maqburī, the Madīnan was Abū Saᶜīd, the father of Saᶜīd al-Maqburī. He was the mawlā of Umm Sharīk and a trustworthy narrator who was firmly established. He died in 100 AH as is in *at-Taqrīb*.

Khālid ibn ᶜAbdullāh. Apparently it is Khālid ibn ᶜAbdullāh ibn ᶜAbd ar-Raḥmān ibn Yazīd aṭ-Ṭaḥḥān Abu'l-Haytham al-Wāsiṭī who narrated from Ismāʿīl ibn Abī Khālid, Ḥumayd aṭ-Ṭawīl, Sulaymān at-Taymī, Abū Isḥāq ash-Shaybānī and others, and from whom Wakīʿ, Ibn Mahdī, Yaḥyā al-Qaṭṭān and others narrated. Ibn Saʿd, Abū Zurʿah, an-Nasāʾī, Abū Ḥātim and at-Tirmidhī regarded him as a trustworthy narrator. He died in 179 AH. That is how it is in *Tahdhīb al-kamāl* by al-Mizzī.

Khālid ibn Asīd. Hishām ibn al-Kalbī said, "He accepted Islam on the day of the Opening [of Makkah to Islam], and he resided in Makkah. He was one of those "whose hearts were reconciled [to Islam]." Ibn Durayd said, "He was a carpenter." It is said that he was lost on the day of al-Yamāmah, but it is said that he died before that, as az-Zurqānī said.

Khālid ibn ʿUqbah ibn Abī Muʿayṭ of Quraysh and [Banī] Umayyah. He was a Companion from those who accepted Islam at the Opening [of Makkah to Islam], and his home was at the marketplace of Madīnah. Az-Zurqānī mentions him.

Khālid ibn al-Walīd ibn al-Mughīrah was the son of the the maternal aunt of Ibn ʿAbbās, and he was Abū Sufyān of Makhzūm. He accepted Islam after Ḥudaybiyyah and before the Opening [of Makkah to Islam], and was present at the battle of Muʾtah. He died in Ḥimṣ in 21 AH, but some say in Madīnah, as is in *Isʿāf al-mubaṭṭaʾ* of as-Suyūṭī.

Khallād ibn as-Sāʾib al-Anṣārī of Banī al-Ḥārith ibn al-Khazraj was a Follower who was a trustworthy narrator. Those who assert that he was a Companion are mistaken, as az-Zurqānī mentioned. His father was as-Sāʾib ibn Khallād (see his entry).

Khansāʾ bint Khidhām. Ibn ʿAbd al-Barr said in *al-Istīʿāb*, "Khansāʾ bint Khidhām ibn Wadīʿah al-Anṣārī of Aws. Her father married her off against her will and the Messenger of Allah ﷺ overturned her marriage. The ḥadīth differ as to her condition at that time. In Mālik's narration from ʿAbd ar-Raḥmān ibn al-Qāsim from his father from ʿAbd ar-Raḥmān and Mujammiʿ from her there is that she was someone who had already been married (*thayyib*). Ibn al-Mubārak mentioned from ath-Thawrī from ᶜAbd ar-Raḥmān ibn al-Qāsim from ᶜAbdullāh ibn Yazīd ibn Wadīᶜah from Khansā᾽ that she was at time a virgin. Mālik's transmission is the correct one. Muḥammad ibn Isḥāq narrated from Ḥajāj ibn as-Sā᾽ib from his father from his grandmother Khansā᾽ that he said, 'She was at that time unmarried to a man and her father married her to a man from Banī ᶜAwf but then she was proposed to by Abū Lubābah ibn ᶜAbd al-Mundhir and her case was raised to the Messenger of Allah ﷺ and he ordered her to let her have her desire and so she married Abū Lubābah."

Khārijah ibn Zayd ibn Thābit was one of the 'seven fuqahā᾽" of Madīnah and one of the greatest of the trustworthy narrators. He died in 99 AH, but some say 100 AH, as Ibn Ḥibbān said. He was the maternal uncle of Saᶜīd as az-Zurqānī said.

Khidhām. Khidām is thus spelt in *al-Fatḥ* and *at-Taqrīb*. Some say that it is Khidhām ibn Wadīᶜah, but others say Ibn Khālid. He was one of the eminent Companions, as az-Zurqānī said, and the father of Khansā᾽.

Kurayb the mawlā of Ibn ᶜAbbās is Ibn Abī Muslim Abū Rushd ibn al-Ḥijāzī whom an-Nasā᾽ī, Ibn Maᶜīn and Ibn Saᶜd regarded as a trustworthy narrator. He died in 98 AH as is in *Isᶜāf al-mubaṭṭa᾽* of as-Suyūṭī.

L

Layth [ḥadīth 263] is ibn Abī Sulaym. Ḥāfiẓ ᶜAbd al-ᶜAẓīm al-Mundhirī said at the end of his book *at-Targhīb wa't-tarhīb*, "There is disagreement about him, and people have narrated from him, but Yaḥyā and an-Nasāʾī regarded him as weak, and Ibn Ḥibbān said, 'He became confused and mixed things up towards the end of his life.' Ad-Dāraquṭnī said, 'He was a man of Sunnah, and they only repudiate his joining together ᶜAṭāʾ, Ṭāwūs and Mujāhid, and nothing else.' Ibn Maᶜīn regarded him as a trustworthy narrator in one narration from him." I have gone to some lengths in writing about his biograpical details in my treatise on visiting the Prophet ﷺ *al-Kalām al-mabrūr fī radd al-qawl al-manṣūr wa radd al-madhhab al-maʾthūr* which is called *as-Saᶜy al-mashkūr* when some people of merit in our age held the opinion that his weakness reached the extent that he could not be used in proof.

M

Maḥmūd ibn Labīd al-Anṣārī al-Ashhalī of Banī ᶜAbd al-Ashhal was born during the life of the Prophet ﷺ and he narrated ḥadīth from the Prophet ﷺ. Muslim mentioned him in the second generation of the Followers *and he did not do anything nor is there known about him what he taught others* [sic][7]. He died in 96 AH. That is how it is in *al-Istīᶜāb.*

Maḥmūd ibn Muḥammad al-Marwazī – by ascription to Marw and the *'z'* is attached to the ascription to distinguish it from *al-marwī* a well known robe worn in ᶜIrāq – ascribed to a sub-section of Kūfa, as as-Samᶜānī said. I have not yet come across biographical material on him so that it can be known whether he is a trustworthy narrator or weak, may Allah graciously bestow the discovery of that upon me.

Makhramah ibn Sulaymān al-Wālibī al-Asadī the Madīnan whom Ibn Maᶜīn regarded as a trustworthy narrator. Al-Wāqidī said, "The Ḥarūriyyah (Khawārij) killed him in 130 AH at Qudayd, as is in *Isᶜāf al-mubaṭṭaʾ* of as-Suyūṭī. He is al-Wālibī by ascription to Wālibah a sub-clan of Asad, as as-Samᶜānī mentioned.

Makḥūl is Abū ᶜAbdullāh al-Hudhalī the Damascene faqīh who narrated many mursal ḥadīth. He narrated from ᶜUbādah, Ubayy, ᶜĀʾishah and the great Companions. Abū Ḥātim said, "I have not seen anyone with more fiqh than Makḥūl." There is a great deal of praise of him and mention that he is one of the trustworthy narrators from the critical scholars of ḥadīth as he expanded in some detail in *Tahdhīb at-tahdhīb,* and in *Tadhkirat al-ḥuffāẓ*. He died in 113 AH, but people say other dates as well.

Mālik ibn ᶜĀmir al-Anṣārī al-Aṣbaḥī was one of the major Followers and a trustworthy narrator. Everyone narrates from him. He died in 74 AH according to the correct position. He is the grandfather of Imām Mālik and the father of Abū Suhayl. As-Suyūṭī and others said thus.

---

[7] I can make no sense of this passage: فلم يصنع شيأً ولا علم منه ما علم غيره

M

Mālik ibn Aws ibn al-Ḥadathān. Ibn al-Athīr said in *Jāmiʿ al-uṣūl,* "Mālik ibn Aws ibn al-Ḥadathān ibn ʿAwf ibn Rabīʿah Abū Saʿīd an-Naṣrī of Banī Naṣr ibn Muʿāwiyah. There is disagreement as to whether or not he was a Companion, but his father was a Companion. Ibn ʿAbd al-Barr said, 'Most people affirm that he was [a Companion].' Ibn Mandah said, 'It is not established.' He narrated from the ten given the good news [of the Garden] and others. He died in Madīnah in 92 AH."

Mālik ibn al-Ḥārith. Adh-Dhahabī said in *al-Kāshif,* "Mālik ibn al-Ḥārith as-Sulamī [narrated] from Abū Saʿīd al-Khudrī and ʿAlqamah an-Nakhaʿī, and from him narrated Manṣūr and al-Aʿmash. He was a trustworthy narrator, and he died in 194 AH."

Manṣūr ibn al-Muʿtamir Abū ʿAttāb as-Sulamī the Kūfan a firmly established trustworthy narrator. He died in 132 AH. From him narrated ath-Thawrī, Shuʿbah, Sulaymān at-Taymī and others. That is how it is in *Jāmiʿ al-uṣūl* by Ibn al-Athīr al-Jazarī and *at-Taqrīb* of Ibn Ḥajar.

Marjānah. See "his mother".

Marwān ibn al-Ḥakam ibn Abi'l-ʿĀṣ ibn Umayyah. It is said that he had seen [the Messenger of Allah ﷺ]. If that is established, yet he does not rise above the rank of someone who is discussed critically. If not, ʿUrwah ibn az-Zubayr said, "Marwān is not suspected in ḥadīth." Sahl ibn Saʿd as-Sāʾidī the Companion narrated depending upon his veracity. They only take revenge on him because he shot Ṭalḥah on the day of the Camel with an arrow and killed him. Later he drew his sword seeking the khilāfah until what happened, happened, as is in *Hady as-sārī: muqaddimah Fatḥ al-bārī* of Ḥāfiẓ Ibn Ḥajar.

The maternal aunt of ʿAbdullāh ibn Abī Bakr. Az-Zurqānī said, "Ibn al-Ḥidhāʾ said, 'She was ʿAmrah bint Ḥazm the maternal aunt of the grandfather of ʿAbdullāh ibn Abī Bakr, and it is said that she was his maternal aunt in a metaphorical sense.' Ḥāfiẓ followed that by saying, 'ʿAmrah was an early Companion, from whom Jābir the Companion narrated, so that then the narration of ᶜAbdullāh from her is interrupted since he did not reach her. The most obvious thing is that what is meant is his actual maternal aunt who was Umm ᶜAmr or Umm Kulthūm.'" The original case must be to interpret it to refer to his actual aunt, and the person who claims that it is used metaphorically must explain the narration along with his claim which necessarily means that the chain of transmission is interrupted, whereas the source contradicts that.

Maymūnah bint al-Ḥārith al-Hilāliyyah whose name had been Barrah, and whom the Messenger of Allah ﷺ named Maymūnah. She died in Sarf in 51 AH, but some say 66 AH and others 63 AH. That is how it is in *al-Istīᶜāb fī aḥwāl al-aṣḥāb* by Ibn ᶜAbd al-Barr.

"Men from the great ones of their people" [hadīth 680]. Ḥāfiẓ Ibn Ḥajar said in the *Muqaddimah Fatḥ al-bārī*, "They were Muḥayyiṣah and Ḥuwayyiṣah the two sons of Masᶜūd, and ᶜAbd ar-Raḥmān and ᶜAbdullāh the two sons of Sahl."

Miḥjan ad-Dīlī of Banī ad-Du᾿il ibn Bakr ibn ᶜAbd Manāf is counted as one of the people of Madīnah, from whom narrated his son Busr ibn Miḥjan, but it is also said Bishr ibn Miḥjan.Abū Nuᶜaym said, "The correct name is Busr." His tribe were Banī ad-Dīl according to al-Kisā᾿ī, Abu ᶜUbayd, Muḥammad ibn Ḥabīb and others, but [Banī] ad-Du᾿il who was Ibn Bakr ibn ᶜAbd Manāf ibn Kinān according to az-Zurqānī. Miḥjan ibn Abī Miḥjan ad-Dīlī was a Companion who had few ḥadīth, as az-Zurqānī said. The spelling of Miḥjan is as spelt out by al-Qārī.

Al-Miqdād ibn ᶜAmr ibn Thaᶜlabah al-Kindī is well known as Ibn al-Aswad. Al-Aswad ibn ᶜAbd Yaghūth adopted him as a son when he was small so that he became known by him [as Ibn al-Aswad]. He was present at Badr and all the other events. He died in 33 AH. That is in *Isᶜāf al-mubaṭṭa᾿* of as-Suyūṭī.

Misᶜar ibn Kidām ibn Ẓahīr al-Hilālī Abū Salamah the Kūfan an eminent, firmly established, trustworthy narrator. He died in 153 AH, but some say 155 AH. It is thus in *Taqrīb at-tahdhīb* and elsewhere.

Al-Miswar ibn Makhramah ibn Nawfal of Quraysh. Both and he and his father were Companions, which he mentioned in *al-Iṣābah* and other books.

Al-Miswar ibn Rifāᶜah ibn Abī Mālik al-Quraẓī by ascription to Banī Qurayẓah a lesser Madīnan Follower who is acceptable. In the *Muwaṭṭaᵓ* he has a single marfūᶜ ḥadīth, but in the six [collections] there is not a single ḥadīth from him. Ibn Ḥibbān regarded him as a trustworthy narrator. He died in 138 AH.

"His mother" [ḥadīth 390] the freed slave [*mawlāh*] of ᶜĀᵓishah ﷺ was Marjānah and she was the mawlāh of ᶜĀᵓishah and an accepted narrator. She was the mother of ᶜAlqamah [ḥadīth 26]. Ibn Ḥibbān regarded her as a trustworthy narrator, as is in *al-Isᶜāf.*

Muᶜādh ibn ᶜAmr ibn Saᶜīd narrating from Muᶜādh from his grandmother [ḥadīth 931]. It is thus in many copies, but the correct chain of transmission is in the *Muwaṭṭaᵓ* of Yaḥyā and its commentary, "Mālik from Zayd ibn Aslam al-ᶜAdawī from ᶜAmr ibn Saᶜd ibn Muᶜādh by ascription to his grandfather since he was ᶜAmr ibn Muᶜādh ibn Saᶜd ibn Muᶜādh al-Ashhalī the Madīnan whose kunyā was Abū Muḥammad.

Muᶜādh ibn Jabal ibn ᶜAmr ibn Aws al-Anṣārī al-Khazrajī Abū ᶜAbd ar-Raḥmān the Madīnan. He was present at al-ᶜAqabah, Badr and all of the major events, and he was one of the four Anṣār who collected the entire Qurᵓān in the life of the Prophet ﷺ. Jābir, Ibn ᶜUmar, Ibn ᶜAbbās, Abū Mūsā and a great number of others narrated from him. He died in the plague of ᶜAmawās in 18 AH as is in *al-Isᶜāf.*

Muᶜādh ibn Saᶜd [ḥadīth 640]. There is a doubt in the ḥadīth as to whether it is Muᶜādh ibn Saᶜd or Saᶜd ibn Muᶜādh. Az-Zurqānī said, "Thus the doubt occurred, and Ibn Mandah and Abū Nuᶜaym mention Muᶜādh ibn Saᶜd among the Companions. He said that in *al-Iṣābah.*"

Muᶜāwiyah ibn Abī Sufyān was Muᶜāwiyah ibn Sakhr ibn Ḥarb ibn Umayyah ibn ᶜAbd Shams ibn ᶜAbd Manāf of Quraysh and Banī Umayyah.

He accepted Islam, he, his father, his brother Yazīd, and his mother Hind bint ᶜUtbah ibn Rabīᶜah ibn ᶜAbd Shams, on the day of the Opening [of Makkah to Islam]. He was one of those "whose hearts were reconciled [*mu᾽allafah qulūbuhum*]", and he made good his Islam, and wrote [the revelation] for the Messenger of Allah ﷺ. When Yazīd his brother died, he [ᶜUmar] appointed him as his [Yazīd's] successor over his governorship in Shām. When ᶜUthmān was appointed khalīfah, he gathered all of Shām under his authority, and it continued like that until ᶜUthmān was killed, and he remained alone in Shām and did not pledge allegiance to ᶜAlī. The battle of Ṣiffīn took place between him and ᶜAlī. All of that is examined in greater detail in *al-Kāmil fi't-tārīkh*. When ᶜAlī was killed, al-Ḥasan [became khalīfah and after negotiations] surrended the amirate [khilāfah] to Muᶜāwiyah. He died in the middle of Rajab in 60 AH, as is in *Asad al-ghābah fī maᶜrifat aṣ-ṣaḥābah* by Ibn al-Athīr al-Jazarī. [See also *Tārīkh al-khulafā᾽* published in English as *The History of the Khalifahs* by Jalal ad-Dīn as-Suyūṭī, Ta-Ha Publishing Ltd., and *al-ᶜAwāṣim min al-qawāṣim* published in English as *Defence Against Disaster* by Qāḍī Abū Bakr ibn al-ᶜArabī, Madīnah Press].

Al-Mubārak ibn Faḍālah Abū Faḍālah – the mawlā of the family of al-Khattāb – al-ᶜAdawī the Baṣran. He was an utterly truthful person who sometimes omitted to mention gaps in his chains of transmission (*mudallis*). Abū Zurᶜah said, "When he says, 'He narrated to us…' he is a trustworthy narrator." He narrated from al-Ḥasan al-Baṣrī and Bakr al-Muznī, and from him narrated Ibn al-Mubārak and others. He died in 166 AH according to the authentic position, as is in *at-Taqrīb* and *al-Kāshif*

Al-Mughīrah aḍ-Ḍabbī was Ibn Miqsam aḍ-Ḍabbī by ascription to Ḍabbah a tribe – their mawlā – Abū Hishām the blind Kūfan. He was a trustworthy narrator who was very exact except that he sometimes omitted to mention gaps in his chains of transmission (*tadlīs*). He narrated from an-Nakhaᶜī, ash-Shaᶜbī and Abū Wā᾽il, and from him narrated Jarīr,

Shuᶜbah, Zāʾidah and others. He died in 136 AH according to the correct opinion, as is in *al-Kāshif* and *at-Taqrīb*.

Al-Mughīrah ibn Ḥakīm narrated from Abū Hurayrah and Ibn ᶜUmar. From him narrated Nāfiᶜ, Ibn Jurayj and Jarīr ibn Ḥāzim. He was a trustworthy narrator. That is how it is in *al-Kāshif* by adh-Dhahabī.

Al-Mughīrah ibn Shuᶜbah ibn Abī ᶜĀmir ibn Masᶜūd ibn Muᶜtab ibn Mālik ibn Kaᶜb ath-Thaqafī whose kunyā was Abū ᶜAbdullāh or Abū ᶜĪsā. He accepted Islam in the year of al-Khandaq and came as an emigrant [to Madīnah]. Some say that the first event he was present at was al-Khandaq. He died in 50 AH in Kūfa. That is how it is in *al-Istīᶜāb*.

Muḥammad [ḥadīth 159] is not Imām Muḥammad, but Abū ᶜAlī aṣ-Ṣawwāf the pupil of Bishr ibn Mūsā al-Asadī. A later copyist gave this chain of transmission.

Muḥammad ibn Abān ibn Ṣāliḥ is one of those whom a large group of critical scholars regard as weak. There is in *Mīzān al-iᶜtidāl* by adh-Dhahabī, "Muḥammad ibn Abān ibn Ṣāliḥ of Quraysh, said to be al-Juᶜfī the Kūfan. He narrated from Zayd ibn Aslam and others. Abū Dāwūd and Ibn Maᶜīn regarded him as weak. Al-Bukhārī said, 'He is not strong.' Someone said he was one of the Murjiʾah." There is in *Lisān al-mīzān* by al-Ḥāfiẓ Ibn Ḥajar, "An-Nasāʾī said, 'Muḥammad ibn Abān ibn Ṣāliḥ of Quraysh was Kūfan, and he is not a trustworthy narrator.' Ibn Ḥibbān said, 'Weak.' Aḥmad said, 'He was not of those who lie.' Ibn Abī Ḥātim said, 'I asked my father about him and he said, "He is not strong. His ḥadīth are to be written down, but he may not be used as a proof."' Al-Bukhārī said in *at-Tārīkh*, 'They say that his memory is not dependable.'"

Muḥammad al-Bāqir ibn ᶜAlī – who [ᶜAlī] was well known as Zayn al-ᶜĀbidīn – ibn Ḥasan ibn ᶜAlī ibn Abī Ṭālib. He was called al-Bāqir because of the vastness [*tabaqqur*] of his knowledge. He died in Madīnah in 118 AH, but some say 119 AH, as is in *at-Taqrīb* and *Jāmiᶜ al-uṣūl*.

Muḥammad ibn ʿAbd ar-Raḥmān ibn Thawbān al-ʿĀmirī the Madīnan whom an-Nasāʾī and ibn Saʿd regarded as a trustworthy narrator and about whom Abū Ḥātim said, "The like of him is not to asked about," as is in *al-Isʿāf*.

Muḥammad ibn ʿAbdullāh ibn ʿAbd ar-Raḥmān ibn Abī Ṣaʿṣaʿah was Abū ʿAbdullāh al-Anṣārī al-Māzinī and he was a trustworthy narrator. He died in 139 AH according to *Isʿāf al-mubaṭṭaʾ* of as-Suyūṭī. He is ascribed to his father, and his grandfather to his [father's] grandfather because he was ʿAbd ar-Raḥmān ibn ʿAbdullāh ibn Abī Ṣaʿṣaʿah.

Muḥammad ibn ʿAbdullāh ibn Nawfal ibn al-Ḥārith ibn ʿAbd al-Muṭṭalib. He was Hāshimī and a Madīnan and was acceptable, as az-Zurqānī said.

Muḥammad ibn Abī Bakr [ibn Muḥammad] ibn ʿAmr ibn Ḥazm. As-Suyūṭī said in *Isʿāf al-mubaṭṭaʾ*, "Muḥammad ibn Abī Bakr [ibn Muḥammad] ibn ʿAmr ibn Ḥazm al-Anṣārī the qāḍī of Madīnah. He narrated from his father Abī Bakr ibn Muḥammad ibn ʿAmr ibn Ḥazm and az-Zuhrī, and from him narrated Mālik and his own son ʿAbd ar-Raḥmān, Shuʿbah, and the two Sufyāns. He died in 132 AH.

Muḥammad ibn Abī Bakr aṣ-Ṣiddīq. His kunyā was Abu'l-Qāsim. After his father died, he grew up in the care of ʿAlī with whom he was present at the battles of the Camel and Ṣiffīn. He was one of the devotees of Quraysh but, however, he also aided in the killing of ʿUthmān [although he stepped back and repented before the actual blow and was not one of the murderers]. ʿUthmān had made him governor of Egypt, and he resided there until Muʿāwiyah sent the armies among whom were ʿAmr ibn al-ʿĀṣ and Muʿāwiyah ibn Khadīj. There was fighting and Muḥammad ibn Abī Bakr was defeated and was killed by Ibn Khadīj in Ṣafar 38 AH, as is in *Tuḥfat al-muḥibbīn fī manāqib al-khulafāʾ ar-rāshidīn*.

Muḥammad ibn Abī Bakr ath-Thaqafī the Ḥijāzī. He was a trustworthy narrator, but he only has this single ḥadīth [386] from Anas, as az-Zurqānī mentioned

M

Muḥammad ibn ʿAlī ibn Abī Ṭālib al-Hāshimī the Madīnan was better known as Ibn al-Ḥanafiyah, and she [al-Ḥanafiyah] was Khawlah of Banī al-Yamāmah, the wife of ʿAlī. Al-ʿIjlī and others regarded him as a trustworthy narrator. He died in 73 AH, as is in *Isʿāf al-mubaṭṭaʾ* of as-Suyūṭī.

Muḥammad ibn ʿAmārah ibn ʿĀmir ibn ʿAmr ibn Ḥazm. Ibn Maʿīn regarded him as a trustworthy narrator, but Abū Ḥātim regarded him as less trustworthy, as as-Suyūṭī said.

Muḥammad ibn ʿAmr ibn ʿAṭāʾ ibn ʿAbbās ibn ʿAlqamah al-ʿĀmirī of Quraysh and a Madīnan was one of the trustworthy narrators of the Followers. He narrated from Abū Ḥumayd, Abū Qatādah and Ibn ʿAbbās, as is in *Jāmiʿ al-uṣūl*.

Muḥammad ibn ʿAmr ibn Ḥalḥalah ad-Duʾalī is Madīnan and Ibn Maʿīn and an-Nasāʾī regarded him as a trustworthy narrator, as is mentioned by as-Suyūṭī. Ad-Duʾalī, but it is also mentioned in *at-Taqrīb* about him that he was ad-Dīlī both of which are by ascription to a tribe.

Muḥammad ibn ʿAmr ibn Ḥazm. Ibn Ḥibbān said in *ath-Thiqāt*, "His kunyā was Abū ʿAbd al-Mālik. He was born in 10 AH during the life of the Prophet ﷺ. He died on the day of al-Ḥarrah in 63 AH. His son Abū Bakr and others narrated from him."

Muḥammad ibn Ibrāhīm ibn al-Ḥārith ibn Khālid at-Taymī Abū ʿAbdullāh the Madīnan. He was a trustworthy narrator. He died in 120 AH according to the most sound position, as is in *at-Taqrīb*. Ibn Maʿīn, Abū Ḥātim, an-Nasāʾī and others regarded him as a trustworthy narrator. Aḥmad said, "There is something in his ḥadīth. He narrates things that are rejected [or unknown]." He died in 120 AH, and he narrates the ḥadīth, "Actions are only by intentions…" in the version of Muḥammad ibn al-Ḥasan. Thus it is in *Isʿāf al-mubaṭṭaʾ* of as-Suyūṭī.

Muḥammad ibn ʿIjlān. Adh-Dhahabī said in *al-Kāshif*, "Muḥammad ibn ʿIjlān the Madīnan the right-acting faqīh [narrated] from his father, Anas and many others. From him narrated Shuʿbah, Mālik, al-Qaṭṭān and many others. Aḥmad and Ibn Maʿīn regarded him as a trustworthy narrator. Others said he had a bad memory. He died in 143 AH."

Muḥammad ibn Jubayr ibn Muṭʿim was Abū Saʿīd al-Qurashī an-Nawfalī. He was a trustworthy narrator and one from whom all transmited. He died at the end of the first century, as az-Zurqānī and others mention.

Muḥammad ibn al-Munkadir ibn ʿAbdullāh ibn al-Hudayr at-Taymī the Madīnan is an eminent trustworthy narrator. He died in 130 AH or after. That is how it is in *at-Taqrīb*.

Muḥammad ibn ʿUqbah the mawlā of az-Zubayr was the brother of Mūsā ibn ʿUqbah the Madīnan. He was a trustworthy narrator as is in *at-Taqrīb*.

Muḥammad ibn Yaḥyā ibn Ḥabbān al-Anṣārī the Madīnan. An-Nasāʾī, Ibn Maʿīn and Abū Ḥātim regarded him as a trustworthy narrator. He died in Madīnah in 121 AH, as is in *Isʿāf al-mubaṭṭaʾ* of as-Suyūṭī. He was a Madīnan faqīh who was a trustworthy narrator. He said, "My grandfather Ḥabbān ibn Munqidh al-Anṣārī al-Māzinī the Companion had...," as az-Zurqānī said.

Muḥammad ibn Zayd at-Taymī was a trustworthy narrator from whom Muslim and the four narrated, as az-Zurqānī mentioned. His mother [ḥadīth 164] was Umm Ḥarām. He said in *at-Taqrīb*, "It is said that her name was Āminah."

Muḥill aḍ-Ḍabbī. Al-Qārī said that it was Miḥill and was the name of a number of ḥadīth scholars. But this is not sufficient in this station. In *at-Taqrīb* there is, "Muḥill ibn Khalīfah aṭ-Ṭāʾī the Kūfan, was a trustworthy narrator of the fourth generation, and Muḥill ibn Muḥriz aḍ-Ḍabbī the Kūfan, in whom there is no harm, is of the sixth. He died in 153 AH." He makes clear that it is spelt 'Muḥill' aḍ-Ḍabbi, about which Muḥammad

Tahir al-Fattanī declared clearly when he said in *al-Mughnī,* "Muḥill ibn Khalīfah is spelt thus – but some say 'Maḥill' – as is Muḥill ibn Muḥriz." Thus al-Qārī's mistake is clear, and the Maker knows best. In *al-Kāshif* of adh-Dhahabī there is, "Muḥill ibn Khalīfah aṭ-Ṭāʾī narrated from his grandfather ᶜAdī ibn Ḥātim and Abu's-Samḥ, and from him narrated Shuᶜbah and Saᶜd Abū Mujāhid. As for Muḥill ibn Muḥriz aḍ-Ḍabbī narrating from ash-Shaᶜbī , he was younger than him."

Mujabbar. See al-Mujabbar.

Al-Mujabbar. He is called al-Mujabbar [the one whose bone was set] because he fell and broke [a limb] and his bone was set. That is what Ibn ᶜAbd al-Barr said. There is in *Jāmiᶜ al-uṣūl,* "Al-Mujabbar ibn ᶜAbd ar-Raḥmān al-Aṣghar ibn ᶜUmar. It is said that his name was ᶜAbd ar-Raḥmān." There is in *Mushtabih an-nisbah* by al-Ḥāfiẓ ᶜAbd al-Ghanī, "Mujabbar. Al-Mujabbar ibn ᶜAbd ar-Raḥmān ibn ᶜUmar ibn al-Khattāb. Mālik narrated from his son ᶜAbd ar-Raḥmān." Az-Zubayr ibn Bakkār said, "He [the father] died while he was in the womb, and so when he was born Ḥafṣah called him after his father, and she said, 'Perhaps, Allah will put his affairs in a good state (*yajburuhu*).'" He said in *al-Istīᶜāb,* "ᶜUmar had three children all of whom were called ᶜAbd ar-Raḥmān, the oldest of whom was a Companion, the middle one of whom was given the kunyā Abū Shaḥmah and he was the one whom his father, ᶜUmar, flogged because of wine, and the third was the father of al-Mujabbar."

Mujāhid was Ibn Jabr Abū al-Ḥajjāj al-Makhzūmī – their mawlā – the Makkan, the Qurʾān teacher, commentator and ḥāfiẓ. He heard Saᶜd, ᶜĀʾishah, Abū Hurayrah, and Ibn ᶜAbbās with whom he spent some time and to whom he recited the Qurʾān. Al-Aᶜmash, Manṣūr, Ibn ᶜAwn, Qatādah and others narrated from him. Qatādah said, "The most knowledgeable of those who remain concerning tafsīr is Mujāhid." Ibn Jurayj said, "That I should have heard from Mujāhid is more beloved to me than my family and my property." He was among the notable trustworthy narrators. That is how it is in *Tadhkirat al-ḥuffāẓ* by adh-

Dhahabī. He mentioned in *at-Taqrīb* and elsewhere that he died either one, two, three or four years after 100 AH.

Mujammi[c] ibn Yazīd ibn Jāriyah al-Anṣārī was one of the great Followers who died om 60 AH.

Mūsā ibn Abī Tamīm the Madīnan. Abū Ḥātim said, "He was a trustworthy narrator in whom there was no harm," as as-Suyūṭī mentioned. Az-Zurqānī said, "In the *Muwaṭṭa᾽* there is only this single marfū[c] ḥadīth [814] from him."

Mūsā ibn Maysarah ad-Dīlī, their mawlā, Abū [c]Urwah the Madīnan was a trustworthy narrator. Mālik used to praise him and describe him as being someone of merit. He died in 133 AH said az-Zurqānī .

Mūsā ibn Sa[c]d ibn Zayd ibn Thābit. Adh-Dhahabī said in *al-Kāshif*, "Mūsā ibn Sa[c]d or Sa[c]īd [narrated] from Sālim and Rabī[c]ah ar-Ra᾽y. From him narrated [c]Umar ibn Muḥammad. He was regarded as a trustworthy narrator." In *at-Taqrīb*, "Mūsā ibn Sa[c]d or Sa[c]īd ibn Zayd ibn Thābit al-Anṣārī the Madīnan is acceptable."

Mūsā ibn [c]Uqbah was a mawlā of the family of az-Zubayr, but it is said that he was a mawlā of Umm Khālid the wife of az-Zubayr. He is a trustworthy narrator. He died in 141 AH, as is in *al-Kāshif*.

Mus[c]ab ibn Sa[c]d ibn Abī Waqqāṣ az-Zuhrī Abū Zurārah the Madīnan is trustworthy and he died in 103 AH. His father was Sa[c]d ibn Abī Waqqāṣ. Thus it is in *Taqrīb at-tahdhīb*.

Muslim ibn Abī Maryam. Abū Dāwūd, an-Nasā᾽ī and Ibn Ma[c]īn regarded him as a trustworthy narrator. He died in the khilāfah of al-Manṣūr, as is mentioned in *al-Is[c]āf*.

Al-Muṭṭalib ibn [c]Abdullāh ibn Ḥanṭab – which occurs in the *Muwaṭṭa᾽* of Yaḥyā as Ḥuwayṭab and is a mistake – and he is Abu'l-Ḥakam al-Muṭṭalib ibn [c]Abdullāh ibn Ḥanṭab ibn al-Ḥārith ibn [c]Ubayd ibn [c]Umar ibn Makhzūm al-Makhzūmī of Quraysh and a Madīnan, one of the trustworthy narrators of the Followers, as is in *Jāmi[c] al-uṣūl*.

M

Al-Muṭṭalib ibn Abī Wadāᶜah as-Sahmī. He was ᶜAbdullāh as-Sahmī, a Companion who accepted Islam on the day of the Opening [of Makkah to Islam]. He resided in Madīnah where he died. His mother was Arwā bint al-Ḥārith ibn ᶜAbd al-Muṭṭalib, and was the daughter of the paternal uncle of the Prophet ﷺ, as az-Zurqānī mentioned.

N

Nāfiʿ. Shaykh al-Islām adh-Dhahabī said in *Tadhkirat al-ḥuffāẓ*, "Nāfiʿ Abū ʿAbdullāh al-ʿAdawī the Madīnan narrated from his mawlā[8] Ibn ʿUmar, ʿĀʾishah, Abū Hurayrah, Umm Salamah, Rāfiʿ ibn Khadīj and a group of others. From him narrated Ayyūb, ʿUbaydullāh, Ibn Jurayj, al-Awzāʿī, Mālik, al-Layth and a large number of people. Al-Bukhārī and others said that the soundest chain of transmission is that of Mālik from Nāfiʿ from Ibn ʿUmar. Ibn Wahb said, 'Mālik narrated to me saying, "I used to go to Nāfiʿ while I was a boy young in years and he would narrate to me. He would sit after the morning prayer in the mosque and hardly anyone could come to him."' Ḥammād ibn Zayd and Muḥammad ibn Saʿd said, 'Nāfiʿ died in 117 AH.' Yaḥyā ibn Maʿīn said, 'Nāfiʿ was Daylamī.' Nāfiʿ said, 'I served Ibn ʿUmar for thirty years, and then Ibn ʿUmar was given thirty thousand dirhams for me and he said, "I fear that the dirhams will be a trial for me," and he set me free.'" (Abridged) There is in *Jāmiʿ al-uṣūl*, "Nāfiʿ ibn Sarjis the mawlā of Ibn ʿUmar was Daylamī and one of the great Madīnan Followers who were famous for ḥadīth. He was one of the trustworthy narrators about whose ḥadīth there is consensus and which are acted upon. The greater part of the ḥadīth of Ibn ʿUmar revolve around him. Mālik said, 'When I heard the ḥadīth of Nāfiʿ from Ibn ʿUmar I could not care whether I heard it from anyone else.' He died in 117 AH, but some say 120 AH." There is the like of that in *Isʿāf al-mubaṭṭaʾbi rijāl* al-*Muwaṭṭaʾ* of as-Suyūṭī because he said, "Nāfiʿ ibn Sarjis ad-Daylamī the mawlā of Ibn ʿUmar the Madīnan narrated from his mawlā (Ibn ʿUmar) and from Rāfiʿ ibn Khadīj, Abū Hurayrah, ʿĀʾishah, Umm Salamah, and others. From him narrated his sons ʿAbdullāh, Abū Bakr, ʿUmar, and az-Zuhrī, Mūsā ibn ʿUqbah, Abū

---

[8] Mawlā means the slave who has been set free. However, both the ex-owner and the ex-slave are the mawlā of each other. The walāʾ relationship includes the ex-owner inheriting from his ex-slave, and his commitment to paying compensatory payments for injuries caused others or in cases of manslaughter.

Ḥanīfah, Mālik, al-Layth and many others." What we know from *ath-Thiqāt* of Ibn Ḥibbān is that Nāfiʿ the mawlā of Ibn ʿUmar was not Ibn Sarjis but someone else, because he said first of all under the letter *nun*, "Nāfiʿ the mawlā of Ibn ʿUmar. Ibn ʿUmar gained him [as spoils] in one battle. His kunyā was Abū ʿAbdullāh, but there is disagreement about his lineage and there is nothing sound about it in my view for me to mention. He narrated from Ibn ʿUmar, Abū Saʿīd, and many people narrated from him. He died in 117 AH." Then later he said, "Nāfiʿ ibn Sarjis al-Ḥijāzī the mawlā of Banī Sibāʿ whose kunyā is Abū Saʿīd. He narrated from Abū Wāqid al-Laythī. There narrated from him ʿAbdullāh ibn ʿUthmān ibn Khashīm." The author of *al-Mishkāh* mentioned in *Asmāʾ rijāl al-Mishkāh* concerning his lineage the like of what is said in *Jāmiʿ al-uṣūl,* [confusing Ibn Sarjis and the mawlā of Ibn ʿUmar] since he said, "Nāfiʿ ibn Sarjis was Daylamī and one of the great Followers. He heard from Ibn ʿUmar and Abū Saʿīd. Many others narrated from him, among them Mālik and az-Zuhrī." He mentioned in *at-Taqrīb* and *at-Tahdhīb* and in *Tahdhīb at-tahdhīb* and *al-Kāshif,* "Nāfiʿ Abū ʿAbdullāh the Madīnan the mawlā of Ibn ʿUmar died in 117 AH," without mentioning his lineage.

Nāfiʿ ibn Jubayr ibn Muṭʿim. He was a trustworthy narrator from whom everyone narrated. He died in 99 AH, as az-Zurqānī mentioned.

Nāfiʿ the mawlā of Abū Qatādah is either Ibn ʿAbbās or Ibn ʿAyyāsh Abū Muḥammad al-Aqraʿ the Madīnan, and he is a trustworthy narrator, and in reality the mawlā of Abū Qatādah, as an-Nasāʾī and al-ʿIjlī mentioned. Ibn Ḥibbān said, "That is said about him because of his attachment to him [Abū Qatādah], and if not then he was the mawlā of ʿUqaylah bint Ṭalq of Ghifār," as is in *Sharḥ az-Zurqānī*.

An-Najāshī was one of the chiefs of the Followers. He accepted Islam but did not emigrate. The Muslims emigrated to him in Abyssinia and he treated them well. The Prophet ﷺ sent ʿAmr ibn Umayyah to him with two letters, the first of which invited him to Islam, and the second of which asked him to marry Umm Ḥabībah to him. He took the letter and placed it upon his eyes and accepted Islam, and he married Umm Ḥabībah to him. ᶜAmr ibn al-ᶜĀṣ accepted Islam at his hands. That is how it is in *Ḍiyāʾ as-sārī*. In *Sharḥ al-Qārī* there is, "An-Najāshī is a name of the ruler of the Ethiopians (Abyssinians) just as one says Chosroes and Caesar for the kings of Persia and Rome. His name was Aṣḥamah." The Prophet ﷺ informed of his death in Rajab of 9 AH.

Negus. See an-Najāshī.

Nuᶜaym ibn ᶜAbdullāh al-Mujmir, the mawlā of ᶜUmar ibn al-Khattāb. He was Abū ᶜAbdullāh the Madīnan whom Ibn Maᶜīn, Abū Ḥātim and others regarded as a trustworthy narrator. Al-Mujmir is an attribute of Nuᶜaym because he used to carry the incense burner [*mijmar*] in front of ᶜUmar ﷺ when he went out to the prayer during Ramaḍān as Ibn Ḥibbān said. Ibn Mākūlā said, "He used to fumigate the mosque with incense." He was a trustworthy narrator from the middlemost of the Followers, as is in *at-Taqrīb*. Nuᶜaym spent twenty years close to Abū Hurayrah and narrated a great deal from him, as is in as-Samᶜānī's *Ansāb*. In *Fatḥ al-bārī* there is, "Both he and his father ᶜAbdullāh were described as that [*Mujmir*] because both of them used to fumigate the mosque of the Prophet ﷺ with incense. One of the people of knowledge claimed that his father was described as that literally but he only metaphorically, but there are views about that."

Nuᶜaym ibn Hazzāl. It is said that he was a Companion, but others say not. His son was Yazīd, as Ibn al-Athīr mentioned in *Asad al-ghābah fī maᶜrifat aṣ-ṣaḥābah* and *Jāmiᶜ al-uṣūl*.

Nubayh ibn Wahb, the brother of ᶜAbd ad-Dār, was ibn Wahb ibn ᶜUthmān al-ᶜAbdarī, the brother of Banī ᶜAbd ad-Dār ibn Qusayy the tribe, i.e. he was one of them. He was one of the younger Followers. He died in 126 AH. His shaykh was ᶜUmar ibn ᶜUbaydullāh ibn Muᶜammar ibn ᶜUthmān ibn ᶜAmr ibn Kaᶜb al-Qurayshi whose grandfather Muᶜammar was a Companion, but who was himself a Follower, as Ibn Ḥibbān mentioned in *ath-Thiqāt*, and as it is similarly in *Sharḥ az-Zurqānī*. Nubayh ibn Wahb ibn ᶜUthmān ibn Abī Ṭalḥah al-Ḥajabī narrated from Abū Hurayrah, Muḥammad ibn al-Ḥanafiyah and Aban ibn ᶜUthmān. From him narrated his sons ᶜAbd al-Aᶜlā, ᶜAbd al-Jabbār, ᶜAbd al-ᶜAzīz as well as Ayyūb ibn Mūsā, Nāfiᶜ, Ibn Isḥāq and a large body of people. An-Nasāʾī and others regarded him as a trustworthy narrator as is in *al-Isᶜāf.*

Nukhaylah is the name of a servant girl of ᶜĀʾishah, as az-Zurqānī said.

An-Nuᶜmān ibn Bashīr al-Anṣārī al-Khazrajī. Both he and his father were Companions. Later he went to live in Shām and then he was appointed amīr of Kūfa. Later he was killed at Ḥimṣ in 65 AH as az-Zurqānī and others said.

Q

Qabīṣah ibn Dhu'ayb ibn Ḥalḥalah al-Khuzā'ī the Madīnan. He was born in the year of the Opening [of Makkah to Islam] and he narrated from 'Uthmān, Ibn 'Awf, Ḥudhayfah, Yazīd ibn Thābit, 'Ā'ishah and Umm Salamah. Az-Zuhrī said, "He was one of the people of knowledge of this ummah." He died in Shām in 87 AH, as is in *Is'āf al-mubaṭṭa'* of as-Suyūṭī. Makḥūl said, "I saw no one more knowledgeable than him in Shām." *Jāmi' al-uṣūl.*

Qābūs. Ḥāfiẓ ibn Ḥajar said in *at-Taqrīb,* "Qābūs ibn Abī Ẓabyān al-Janbī the Kūfan who has in him some weakness." There is in *al-Ansāb* of as-Sam'ānī, "Al-Janbī is by ascription to Janb a number of tribes, but some say to a tribe of Madhḥij, to whom Abū Ẓabyān al-Janbī is ascribed. His personal name is Ḥuṣayn ibn Jundub. He narrated from 'Alī ﷺ and Ibn Mas'ūd. His son was Qābūs ibn Abī Ẓabyān al-Janbī." (Abridged)

Al-Qa'qa' ibn Ḥakīm. He was from Kinānah and was a Madīnan who was a trustworthy narrator. He mentioned him in *al-Kāshif.*

Al-Qāsim ibn Muḥammad ibn Abī Bakr aṣ-Ṣiddīq the Madīnan. Ibn Sa'd said that he was an eminent trustworthy narrator, a scrupulous faqīh and 'ālim. He died in 106 AH according to the sound position. That is what as-Suyūṭī and others said.

Qatādah ibn Di'āmah – as al-Fattanī spelt it in *al-Mughnī* – ibn Qatādah ibn 'Azīz Abu'l-Khattāb as-Sadūsī the blind Baṣran Qur'ānic commentator – he was born blind. He narrated from Anas ﷺ, 'Abdullāh ibn Sarjis ﷺ, Sa'īd ibn al-Musayyab and others, and from him narrated Mis'ar, Abū 'Awānah, Hishām ad-Dastawā'ī, Sa'īd ibn Abī 'Arūbah and others. Ibn Sīrīn said, "He had the greatest capacity for memorisation of people." Aḥmad said, "He was knowledgeable of the Qur'ānic commentary [*tafsīr*] and of the disagreements of the people of knowledge," and he described him as having powers of memory and knowledge of fiqh and he went to great lengths in his mention of him. He was one of the most magnificent of the trustworthy narrators, well versed in Arabic and the dialects, the history of the Arabs and their genealogies. He died in the plague in Wāsiṭ in 118 AH, but some say 117 AH. That is how it is in the *Tadhkirat al-ḥuffāẓ* by adh-Dhahabī and there is a lengthy and comprehensive biographical notice comprising people's praise of him in *Tahdhīb at-tahdhīb* and elsewhere.

Qays ibn Abī Ḥāzim is Abū ᶜAbdullāh al-Bajalī the Kūfan and major Follower. He emigrated to the Prophet ﷺ but missed being a Companion by a single night. He narrated from Abū Bakr, ᶜUmar and others. From him narrated Bayān ibn Bishr, Ismāᶜīl ibn Abī Khālid and a great number of other people, and they regarded him as a trustworthy narrator. It is said that he he united in himself to have narrated from the ten men promised [the Garden]. He died after or before 90 AH having exceeded a hundred years in age. Thus it is in *at-Taqrīb* and *al-Kāshif.* Ibn al-Athīr mentioned in *Jāmiᶜ al-uṣūl* that he narrated from the ten given the good news [of the Garden] except for ᶜAbd ar-Raḥmān ibn ᶜAwf. Ibn ᶜUyaynah said, "There was not in Kūfa anyone who narrated more from the Companions of the Prophet ﷺ than Qays ibn Abī Ḥāzim." Abū Ḥāzim's name was Ḥuṣayn ibn ᶜAwn, but it is also said that it was ᶜAwf ibn al-Ḥārith, and some say ᶜAwf ibn al-Ḥārith of Banī Aslam ibn Aḥmas ibn al-Ghawth ibn Anmār al-Aḥmasī al-Bajalī.

Qays ibn ar-Rabīᶜ al-Asadī – by ascription to Asad. He was a trustworthy narrator whom Shuᶜbah and Sufyān regarded as such. It is narrated of Ibn ᶜUyaynah, "I have not seen in Kūfa anyone better in ḥadīth than him," but Wakīᶜ and others regarded him as weak in ḥadīth. Ibn ᶜAwn said, "The generality of his narrations are straight, and the right position respecting him is that of Shuᶜbah, and there is no harm in him." He died in 107 AH, and people have said other dates, as is in *Tahdhīb at-tahdhīb.*

Qudāmah ibn Maẓᶜūn ibn Ḥabīb ibn Wahb ibn Ḥudhāfah ibn Jumaḥ of Quraysh and Jumaḥ. He was the maternal uncle of ᶜAbdullāh and Ḥafṣah the son and daughter of ᶜUmar ibn al-Khattāb. He emigrated to

Abyssinia with his two brothers ʿUthmān ibn Maẓʿūn and ʿAbdullāh ibn Maẓʿūn, and was then later present at Badr and the rest of the events. He died in 36 AH, as is in *al-Istīʿāb*.

R

Rabīᶜah ibn ᶜAbdullāh ibn al-Hudayr at-Taymī the Madīnan. He narrated from ᶜUmar, Ṭalḥah, Abū Saᶜīd al-Khudrī, and from him narrated his brother's two sons Muḥammad and Abū Bakr – both sons of al-Munkadir ibn ᶜAbdullāh – and Ibn Abī Mulaykah. Ibn Ḥibbān mentioned him in *ath-Thiqāt.* Ibn Saᶜd said, "He was born at the time of the Messenger of Allah ﷺ and he was a trustworthy narrator who narrated few ḥadīth." Al-ᶜIjlī said, "A Madīnan Follower who was a trustworthy narrator. He died in 93 AH." That is how it is in *Tahdhīb at-tahdhīb*.

Rabīᶜah ar-Raʾy – the shaykh of Mālik – ibn Abī ᶜAbd ar-Raḥmān Farrūkh at-Taymī Abū ᶜUthmān, but some say Abū ᶜAbd ar-Raḥmān, a pre-eminent Follower, one of the fuqahāʾ of Madīnah. He heard from Anas ibn Mālik and as-Sāʾib ibn Yazīd. Ath-Thawri and Mālik narrated from him. He was Madīnan, a faqīh and one of the notables. Aḥmad said he was a trustworthy narrator, and Yaᶜqūb ibn Shaybah said that he was a firmly established trustworthy narrator. He died in 136 AH, as is in *Isᶜāf al-mubaṭṭaʾ* of as-Suyūṭī.

Ar-Rabīᶜ ibn Ṣabīḥ as-Saᶜdī al-Baṣrī was an utterly truthful man who had a bad memory. He was a devout worshipper and a mujāhid. Ar-Rāmahurmuzī said, "He was the first person in Baṣra to compile a book." He died in 160 AH. That is how it is in *at-Taqrīb*. He mentioned in *Tahdhīb at-tahdhīb* that he narrated from al-Ḥasan al-Baṣrī, Ḥumayd aṭ-Ṭawīl, Yazīd ar-Raqāshī, Abu'z-Zubayr, Abū Ghālib and others. From him narrated ath-Thawrī, Ibn al-Mubārak, Wakīᶜ and others. Al-ᶜIjlī and Ibn ᶜAdī said there is no harm in him.

Rāfiᶜ ibn Khadīj was a well known Companion who was present at Uḥud and everything after it. He died at the beginning of 74 AH, as as-Suyūṭī mentioned.

Rajāʾ ibn Ḥaywah. He said in *at-Taqrīb,* "Rajāʾ ibn Ḥaywah al-Kindī al-Filisṭīnī was a trustworthy narrator and a faqīh. He died in 112 AH."

S

Aṣ-Ṣaʿb ibn Jaththāmah ibn Qays ibn Rabīʿah al-Laythī was one of the major Companions and he died during the khilāfah of ʿUthmān according to the most correct view.

Ṣadaqah ibn Yasār. ʿAbdullāh ibn Aḥmad said [narrating] from his father, "He is one of the trustworthy narrators." Ibn Maʿīn said he was a trustworthy narrator, and Abū Ḥātim said that he was a right-acting person. Al-Ājurrī said [narrating] from Abū Dāwūd, "He was a trustworthy narrator." I asked, "One of the people of Makkah?" He said, "One of the people of al-Jazīrah who resided in Makkah." That is how it is in *Tahdhīb at-tahdhīb*.

Saʿd ibn Abī Waqqāṣ Mālik ibn Wahb ibn ʿAbd Manāf ibn Zuhrah ibn Kilāb az-Zuhrī Abū Isḥāq was one of the ten who were promised the Garden, and whose merits are numerous and who was the last of the ten to die, dying, according to the most well know position, in 55 AH. Thus it is in *Taqrīb at-tahdhīb*.

Saʿd ibn Isḥāq ibn Kaʿb ibn ʿUjrah. As-Suyūṭī said in *al-Isʿāf*, "Saʿd ibn Isḥāq ibn Kaʿb ibn ʿUjrah al-Quḍāʿī the Madīnan was an ally of the Anṣār. Ibn Maʿīn, an-Nasāʾī and others regarded him as a trustworthy narrator. He died after 140 AH. His aunt was Zaynab bint Kaʿb, the wife of Abū Saʿīd al-Khudrī, whom Ibn Ḥibbān regarded as a trustworthy narrator.

Ṣafiyyah is the Umm al-Muʾminin Ṣafiyyah bint Ḥuyayy ibn Akhṭab ibn Saʿyah of the Children of Isrāʾīl of the tribe of Hārūn ibn ʿImrān the brother of Mūsā. Her husband, Kinānah, was killed in the battle of Khaybar when the Messenger of Allah ﷺ opened it [to Islam] in 7 AH. She fell among the captives and the Messenger of Allah ﷺ chose her for himself. She accepted Islam and he freed and married her. She[9] died in 52 AH, but some say other things, as Ibn al-Athīr mentioned.

---

[9] Text has mistakenly, "He died."

S

Ṣafiyyah bint Abī ᶜUbayd the wife of ᶜAbdullāh ibn ᶜUmar whom he married in the lifetime of her father, and ᶜUmar gave her a dowry on his behalf of four hundred dirhams. She bore him Wāqid, Abū Bakr, Abū ᶜUbaydah, ᶜUbaydullāh, ᶜUmar, Ḥafṣah and Sawdah. Ibn Mandah said, "She reached [to meet] the Prophet ﷺ but did not hear anything from him." But ad-Dāraquṭnī rejected that. Al-ᶜIjlī and Ibn Ḥibbān mentioned her as one of the trustworthy narrators of the Followers. So says az-Zurqānī.

Ṣafwān ibn ᶜAbdullāh ibn Ṣafwān ibn Umayyah al-Jumaḥī the Makkan who was one of the Followers. Al-ᶜIjlī said he was a trustworthy narrator. His grandfather Ṣafwān was the man of the story [in ḥadīth 684]. He died during the days in which ᶜUthmān was killed, as is in *Isᶜāf al-mubaṭṭaʾ* of as-Suyūṭī and in *at-Taqrīb*.

Ṣafwān ibn Umayyah was the grandfather of Ṣafwān ibn ᶜAbdullāh. He was ibn Umayyah ibn Khalf ibn Wahb ibn Qudāmah ibn Jumaḥ of Quraysh, the Companion, who was one of those whose hearts were reconciled to Islam.

Sahl ibn ᶜAbbās at-Tirmidhī by ascription to Tirmidh or Turmidh or Tarmidh, but the former is the well known [version], a city near to Balkh as as-Samᶜānī said. Adh-Dhahabī said in *Mīzān al-iᶜtidāl*, "Ad-Dāraquṭnī abandoned [narrating from] him, and he said, 'He is not a trustworthy narrator.'"

Sahl ibn Abī Ḥathmah is Abū ᶜAbd ar-Raḥmān, but some say Abū Yaḥyā, Sahl ibn Abī Ḥathmah al-Anṣārī the Madīnan. The name of Abū Ḥathmah was ᶜAbdullāh, but some say ᶜĀmir, ibn Sāᶜidah ibn ᶜĀmir ibn ᶜAdī a younger Companion who pledged allegiance under the tree [at al-Ḥudaybiyah] and who was present at all the battles except for Badr, as Ibn Abī Ḥātim said. Ibn al-Qaṭṭān said, "This is not correct." Ibn Ḥibbān, al-Wāqidī, Abū Jaᶜfar aṭ-Ṭabarī, Ibn as-Sakan, al-Ḥākim and others said that he was a boy of eight when the Prophet ﷺ died. Adh-Dhahabī mentioned that he died in the khilāfah of Muᶜāwiyah, as is in *Tahdhīb at-tahdhīb, Taqrīb at-tahdhīb, Jāmiᶜ al-uṣūl* and elsewhere.

Sahl ibn Saᶜd as-Sāʾidī – by ascription to Sāᶜidah ibn Kaᶜb ibn al-Khazraj, a tribe of the Anṣār which as-Suyūṭī mentions in *Lubb al-lubāb fi taḥrīr al-ansāb*. He was the last of the Companions to die in Madīnah. He died in 88 AH, but some say 91 AH, as is in *Isᶜāf al-mubaṭṭaʾ* of as-Suyūṭī.

Saᶜīd ibn Abī ᶜArūbah – whose name was Mihrān [i.e. Abū ᶜArūbah's] – al-ᶜAdawī being a mawlā of Banī ᶜAdī ibn Yashkur, Abu'n-Naḍr the Baṣran. Ibn Maᶜīn, an-Nasāʾī and Abū Zurᶜah said he was a trustworthy narrator, and Ibn Abī Khaythamah said, "The most firmly established of people in [narrating from] Qatādah were Saᶜīd ibn Abī ᶜArūbah and Hishām ad-Dastawāʾī." Abū Dāwūd aṭ-Ṭayālisī said, "He was the one who memorised most from among the companions of Qatādah." Abū Ḥātim said, "He was, before he confused things, a trustworthy narrator." Ibn Ḥibbān mentioned him in *ath-Thiqāt,* and he said that he died in 155 AH, and that he remained in a state wherein he mixed things up for five years. That is how it is in *Tahdhīb at-tahdhīb*.

Saᶜīd – some say that he was Saᶜd – ibn ᶜAmr ibn Sulaym az-Zuraqī al-Anṣārī. Ibn Maᶜīn and Ibn Ḥibbān regarded him as a trustworthy narrator. He died in 134 AH. Ibn ᶜAbd al-Barr said, "He has no other ḥadīth than this one [564] in the *Muwaṭṭaʾ*," as az-Zurqānī and al-Qārī said.

Saᶜīd ibn Hishām. It is thus we find it in the copies we have. What is in *Tahdhīb al-kamāl* and its *Tahdhīb* and in its *Taqrīb* and its *Tadhhib* and in *al-Kāshif,* the *Jāmiᶜ al-uṣūl* and in the book *ath-Thiqāt* by Ibn Ḥibbān is that his name was Saᶜd ibn Hishām ibn ᶜĀmir al-Anṣārī the Madīnan, the son of Anas' paternal uncle. He narrated from his father, ᶜĀʾishah, Ibn ᶜAbbās, Samurah, Anas and others, and from him narrated Zurārah and al-Ḥasan al-Baṣrī. An-Nasāʾī and Ibn Saᶜd declared him to be a trustworthy narrator. He became a shahīd at Mukrān, a place in India. That is how it is in the book *al-Ḥujjaj*.

Sa^c^īd ibn Jubayr is Abū ^c^Abdullāh the Kūfan and one of the noted imāms. When the people of Kūfa used to come to Ibn ^c^Abbās to ask for fatwās he would say, "Is Sa^c^īd ibn Jubayr not among you?" Al-Ḥajjāj killed him in Sha^c^bān 95 AH, as is in *Is^c^āf al-mubaṭṭa^ɔ^* of as-Suyūṭī.

Sa^c^īd ibn al-Musayyab is Abū Muḥammad al-Makhzūmī of Quraysh the Madīnan, and one of the chiefs of the Followers. Makḥūl said, "I went around the whole land but I didn't meet anyone more knowledgeable than Ibn al-Musayyab." He was born two years into the khilāfah of ^c^Umar and died in 93 AH. That is how the author of *al-Mishkāh* mentioned him in *Asmā^ɔ^ rijāl al-mishkāh.* He was the lord of the fuqahā^ɔ^ of the Followers. Qatādah said, "I saw no one more knowledgeable of the ḥalāl and the ḥarām than him." That is how it is in *Is^c^āf al-mubaṭṭa^ɔ^* of as-Suyūṭī.

Sa^c^īd ibn Sulaymān ibn Zayd ibn Thābit. He was one of the narrators whom everyone used and one of the trustworthy narrators, as az-Zurqānī said.

Sa^c^īd [207] is ibn Yasār the Madīnan Follower who was a trustworthy narrator. He died in 117 AH, but some say a year before that. Everyone narrates from him as is in the *Sharḥ* of az-Zurqānī .

Sa^c^īd al-Jārī ibn al-Jār. This is how it is found in many copies, and in the *Muwaṭṭa^ɔ^* of Yaḥyā it is from Sa^c^īd al-Jārī the mawlā of ^c^Umar ibn al-Khattāb. As-Sam^c^ānī mentioned about his name that it was Sa^c^d without a *yā* [i.e. not Sa^c^īd] when he said that al-Jārī is by ascription to al-Jār which is an area on the coast near to the prophetic Madīnah, and the one ascribed to it is Sa^c^d ibn Nawfal al-Jārī who was ^c^Umar's governor. He narrated from Abū Hurayrah and ^c^Abdullāh ibn ^c^Umar and from him narrated Zayd ibn Aslam." Ibn al-Athīr named him similarly in *Jāmi^c^ al-uṣūl.*

Sa^c^īd al-Maqburī or al-Maqbarī. He used to reside near a graveyard [*maqbarah*] and was thus ascribed to it [in his name]. He mixed things up four years before his death, and Mālik and the like of him had heard from him before that, says az-Zurqānī . His name was Saʿīd ibn Abī Saʿīd Kaysān the Madīnan. They agree that he is a trustworthy narrator. He died in 123 AH. That is how it is in *Isʿāf al-mubaṭṭaʾ* of as-Suyūṭī. He was Saʿīd Abū Saʿīd, and he was a Madīnan who was a trustworthy narrator. He died at the end of the twenties [after the first century] or a little before it, as it is an *at-Taqrīb*. For his father [ḥadīth 310] see Kaysān ibn Saʿīd al-Maqburī.

Saʿīd ar-Raqāshī by ascription to Raqāsh the name of a woman who had so many children that they became a tribe, and she was the daughter of Sabīʿah ibn Qays ibn Thaʿlabah. As-Samʿānī and Ibn al-Athīr mentioned him. This Saʿīd is probably Saʿīd ibn ʿAbd ar-Raḥmān ar-Raqāshī whom adh-Dhahabī mentioned in *Mīzān al-iʿtidāl* and said, "Yaḥyā ibn al-Qaṭṭān regarded him as soft, but a group regard him as a trustworthy narrator. Ibn ʿAdī said, 'Ibn al-Qaṭṭān hesitated over him, but I see no harm in him.' It is narrated of Ibn Sīrīn that ʿUmar ibn al-Khattāb said, 'Have taqwā of Allah and have taqwā [be wary] of people.'" I myself [Shaykh ʿAbd al-Ḥayy] think that this is a mistake from the copiests for I found this exact same narration in the Book of Ḥajj in which is, "Muḥammad [said], 'Ar-Rabīʿ ibn Ṣabīḥ al-Baṣrī informed us from Yazīd ar-Raqāshī [see his entry] from Anas and from al-Ḥasan al-Baṣrī both of whom ascribed it directly [to the Prophet ﷺ]...'"

Salamah ibn Ṣafwān ibn Salamah az-Zuraqī – by ascription to Banī Zurayq – was a trustworthy Madīnan narrator.

Ṣāliḥ ibn Abī Ṣāliḥ Nabhān al-Madīnī. He narrated from Ibn ʿAbbās, ʿĀʾishah, Abū Hurayrah and others. From him narrated Ibn Abī Dhiʾb, Ibn Jurayj, the two Sufyāns and others. Bishr ibn ʿUmar said, "I asked Mālik about him and he said, 'He is not trustworthy.'" Aḥmad ibn Ḥanbal said, "It is as if Mālik reached him when he became confused and mixed things up. Those who heard from him before that, then that [is acceptable]. The great ones of the people of Madīnah narrated from him and his ḥadīth are fine, and I know nothing bad about him." Aḥmad ibn Saʿīd ibn Abī Maryam said, "I heard Ibn Maᶜīn saying, 'Ṣāliḥ the mawlā of at-Tawᵓamah (the twin) is trustworthy and a decisive argument.' I said, 'Mālik gave up listening to him.' He answered, 'Mālik only reached him after he had aged and was in his dotage.'" Al-Jūzajānī said, "He changed later in life, but the ḥadīth of Ibn Abī Dhiᵓb from him are acceptable because he listened to him of old, but ath-Thawrī listened to him after he had altered." Ibn ᶜAdī said, "There is no harm in him, when the older ones narrate from him such as Ibn Abī Dhiᵓb, Ibn Jurayj and Ziyād ibn Saᶜd." Al-ᶜIjlī said, "A Follower who is trustworthy." He died in 125 AH. That is how it is in *Tahdhīb at-tahdhīb.*

Ṣāliḥ ibn Kaysān. He was the Madīnan mawlā of Ghifār, whom Aḥmad and Ibn Maᶜīn regarded as a trustworthy narrator. He died after 140 AH, as is in *al-Isᶜāf.*

Sālim Abu'n-Naḍr the Madīnan. See him under Abu'n-Naḍr.

Sālim ibn ᶜAbdullāh Ibn ᶜUmar Abū ᶜAmr or Abū ᶜAbdullāh was Madīnan and a faqīh. Mālik said, "No one in his time more resembled those who had passed away of the right-acting people in terms of doing-without [*zuhd*] and merit, than he did." Aḥmad ibn Ḥanbal and Isḥāq ibn Rāhwayh said, "The soundest chain of transmission is Ibn Shihāb az-Zuhrī from Sālim from his father." Al-ᶜIjlī said, "A Madīnan Follower who was trustworthy, he died in 106 AH according to the soundest view." His father was ᶜAbdullāh ibn ᶜUmar ibn al-Khattāb.

Sallām ibn Sulaym al-Ḥanafī by ascription to the tribe of Banī Ḥanīfah. As-Samᶜānī said in *al-Ansāb,* "Ḥanafī by ascription to Banī Ḥanīfah, a people the majority of whom resided in al-Yamāmah and who had followed Musaylimah the Liar who claimed to be a prophet. Then later they accepted Islam in the time of Abū Bakr. It is well known that a large body of people are ascribed to them." There is in *Tahdhīb at-tahdhīb,* "Sallām ibn Sulaym al-Ḥanafī their mawlā Abu'l-Aḥwaṣ the Kūfan narrated from Abū Isḥāq as-Sabīᶜī, Sammāk ibn Ḥarb, Ziyād ibn ᶜAlāqah, al-Aswad ibn Qays, Manṣūr and others. From him narrated Wakīᶜ, Ibn Mahdī,

Abū Nuᶜaym, Saᶜīd ibn Manṣūr and others. Al-ᶜIjlī said, 'He was trustworthy, a person of the Sunnah and following.' Abū Zurᶜah and an-Nasāʾī said, 'Trustworthy.' Ibn Ḥibbān mentioned him in *ath-Thiqāt*. Al-Bukhārī said, 'ᶜAbdullāh ibn Abi'l-Aswad narrated to me saying, "He died in 79" meaning after the century [179 AH].'" (Abridged) There is in al-Fattanī's *Mughni*, "Sallām: everyone [with that name] is with a doubled [lam] except for ᶜAbdullāh ibn Salām [the Companion], and Abū ᶜAbdullāh Muḥammad ibn Salām the shaykh of al-Bukhārī, but a group of people spell it with a doubling [of the lam]. Apart from in the two ṣaḥīḥ books there are another three: Salām ibn Muḥammad, Muḥammad ibn ᶜAbd al-Wahhāb ibn Salām and Salām ibn Abi'l-Ḥaqīq." There is also in it, "Sulaym [with the letters sīn, lām, yā, mīm]: everyone [with that name] has it spelled with *ḍamm* ['u' on the first letter] except for Salīm ibn Ḥayyān." I saw in the *Sharḥ al-Qārī* that he explains the ascription of him being Ḥanafī as his saying, "He is ascribed to Abū Ḥanīfah, with omission of the extra letters [the yā and tā marbūṭah] as in the case of *al-faraḍi* [as an adjective from *farīḍah*]."And this is an obvious mistake, and it is thought that it originates from one of the transcribers of his book and not from him.

Shaqīq ibn Salamah ibn Wāʾil, al-Asadī by ascription to Asad, the name of a number of tribes.

Ash-Sharīd ibn Suwayd ath-Thaqafī was a Companion who was present at the pledge of allegiance of Riḍwān.

Sharīk ibn ᶜAbdullāh ibn Abī Numayr, Abū ᶜAbdullāh the Madīnan. Ibn Saᶜd and Abū Dāwūd regarded him as a trustworthy narrator. Ibn Maᶜīn and an-Nasāʾī said that there is no harm in him. Ibn ᶜAdī said, "When a trustworthy narrator narrates from him there is no harm in him. That is how it is in *Hady as-sārī* the introduction to *Fatḥ al-bārī* by al-Ḥāfiẓ Ibn Ḥajar. In Yaḥyā's copy it is Abū Namīr and the spelling is according to az-Zurqānī .

Shaykh Abū ᶜAlī [118] the author's shaykh. I [Shaykh ᶜAbd al-Ḥayy] have not yet come across biographical material on him [or Maḥmūd ibn Muḥammad al-Marwazī] so that it can be known whether they are trustworthy narrators or weak narrators, may Allah graciously bestow the discovery of that upon me.[10]

Ash-Shifāʾ was Bint ᶜAbdullāh ibn ᶜAbd Shams ibn Khālid of Quraysh al-ᶜAdawiyyah and one of the women who pledged allegiance. Aḥmad ibn Ṣāliḥ said, "Her name was Laylā but ash-Shifāʾ was used more often," as is in *al-Istiᶜāb.*

Shuᶜbah ibn al-Ḥajjāj ibn al-Ward al-ᶜItkī – their mawlā – Abū Bisṭām of Wāsiṭ and Baṣra. He was a trustworthy narrator and a thorough ḥāfiẓ. Ath-Thawrī used to say, "He is the Amīr al-Muʾminīn in ḥadīth." He died in 120 AH. His shaykh was al-Ḥakam ibn ᶜUtbah according to the copies of this book or ᶜUtaybah according to the Ḥāfiẓ in *at-Taqrīb* and he was a firmly established trustworthy narrator who was one of the greatest companions of an-Nakhaᶜī.

Shurayḥ is Ibn al-Ḥārith ibn Qays the qāḍī Abū Umayyah al-Kindī the Kūfan. [ḥadīth 575]. It is said that it is Shurayḥ ibn Sharaḥbīl one of the trustworthy narrators of the eminent men who had lived in both the Jāhiliyyah and Islam. ᶜUmar made him the qāḍī of Kūfa and then later ᶜAlī. Then after him he withdrew from post of qāḍī a year before his death in the time of al-Ḥajjāj. He lived for 120 years, and died in 78 AH, but some say 80 AH. Ibn Maᶜīn and others regarded him as a trustworthy narrator, as is in *Tadhkirat al-ḥuffāẓ* of adh-Dhahabī.

[10] This ḥadīth is not a narration of Muḥammad ibn al-Ḥasan and is not to be found in authentic copies.... It is a ḥadīth that is only to be found in a copy of Abū ᶜAlī aṣ-Ṣawwāf which has been entered into the text by mistake by some copyists. This Abū ᶜAlī is not a shaykh of the author's, but rather he is aṣ-Ṣawwāf, Muḥammad ibn Aḥmad ibn al-Ḥasan aṣ-Ṣawwāf who is a narrator from the fourth century whose shaykh was al-Marwazī whose biography is in *Tārīkh Baghdād* by al-Khaṭīb.

Ṣilah ibn Zufar was Abu'l-ᶜAlāʾ al-ᶜAbsī the Kūfan who narrated from ᶜAmmār, Ḥudhayfah, Ibn Masᶜūd, ᶜAlī and Ibn ᶜAbbās, and from whom narrated Abū Wāʾil, Abū Isḥāq as-Sabīᶜī, Ayyūb as-Sakhtiyānī and others. Al-Khaṭīb, Ibn Kharrāsh and Ibn Ḥibbān said that he was a trustworthy narrator, and similarly it is narrated of Ibn Maᶜīn, al-ᶜIjlī and Ibn Numayr. He died during the khilāfah of Musᶜab ibn az-Zubayr, as is in *Tahdhīb at-tahdhīb*.

A son of Saᶜd ibn Abī Waqqāṣ [ḥadīth 126]. Ibn ᶜAbd al-Barr said in *al-Istidhkār*, "This ḥadīth is interrupted and is not sound."

Sufyān ibn ᶜUyaynah is the ḥāfiẓ and Shaykh al-Islām, Abū Muḥammad Sufyān ibn Abī Zuhayr. Ibn al-Madīnī and Khalīfah said, "The name of his father was al-Fard, but some say it was Numayr ibn ᶜAbdullāh ibn Mālik, and he is called an-Numayrī because he was one of the children of an-Nimr ibn ᶜUthmān ibn Naṣr ibn Zahrān who came to reside in Madīnah, and he was a man from Azd, Shanūʾah ibn al-Ghawth ibn Nabt ibn Mālik ibn Zayd ibn Kahlān ibn Sabāʾ the well known tribe, as az-Zurqānī mentioned.

Sufyān ibn ᶜUyaynah al-Hilālī the Kūfan, the ḥadīth scholar of the Ḥaram in Makkah. He was born in 107 AH, and heard from az-Zuhrī, Zayd ibn Aslam, Manṣūr ibn al-Muᶜtamir and others. From him narrated al-Aᶜmash, Shuᶜbah, Ibn Jurayj, Ibn al-Mubārak, ash-Shāfiᶜī, Aḥmad, Yaḥyā ibn Maᶜīn, Isḥāq ibn Rāhwayh and innumerable others. Adh-Dhahabī said in *Tadhkirat al-ḥuffāẓ*, "He was an imām, a decisive proof, a ḥāfiẓ, with vast knowledge and a great rank. Ash-Shāfiᶜī said, 'If it had not been for Mālik and Sufyān the knowledge of the Ḥijāz would have gone.' Al-ᶜIjlī said, 'He was firmly established in ḥadīth.' Ibn Maᶜīn said, 'He was the most firmly established in [narrating from] ᶜAmr ibn Dīnār, and the imāms agree on using him as a decisive proof.' He performed the Ḥajj seventy times, and died in 198 AH." (Abridged)

Sufyān ath-Thawrī is Abū ᶜAbdullāh Sufyān ibn Saᶜīd ibn Masrūq ath-Thawrī the Kūfan by ascription to Thawr – ibn ᶜAbd Manāt ibn Add ibn Ṭānijah a tribe. He narrated from many people and in turn many narrated from him as al-Mizzī explained in detail in *Tahdhīb al-kamāl*. He mentioned in his biographical notice that "Shuᶜbah, Ibn ᶜUyaynah, Abū ᶜĀṣim and Ibn Maᶜīn all said that he was the Amīr al-Muʾminīn in ḥadīth. Ibn al-Mubārak said, 'I wrote down [ḥadīth] from one thousand one hundred shaykhs. I did not write down from anyone better than Sufyān.' Shuᶜbah said, 'Sufyān has a better memory than me.' Ibn Mahdī said, 'Wahb used to prefer Sufyān over Mālik for his memorisation.' Ad-Dūrī said, 'I saw that Yaḥyā ibn Maᶜīn did not prefer anyone over Sufyān in his age with respect to fiqh, ḥadīth, doing without or anything.' He was born in 97 AH, and died in Baṣra in 161 AH." (Abridged.)

Suhayl ibn Abī Ṣāliḥ. Ibn Suhayl ibn Abī Ṣāliḥ is how we find it in one of the copies, but in some others it is Suhayl ibn Abī Ṣāliḥ, and in two corrected copies it is Ibn Abī Ṣāliḥ, and this is the correct position which agrees with the narration of "Yaḥyā from Mālik from Suhayl ibn Abī Ṣāliḥ from his father…" Perhaps the "ibn" in addition to the name Suhayl in the first copy is one of the additions of the copyist, because this narration is from Suhayl ibn Abī Ṣāliḥ and not from his son nor is it to Suhayl ibn Abī Ṣāliḥ ibn Abī Ṣāliḥ. He is Suhayl ibn Abī Ṣāliḥ Abū Yazīd the Madīnan whom Ibn Ḥibbān mentioned in *ath-Thiqāt*. Ibn Saᶜd said, "He was a trustworthy narrator who had many ḥadīth." Al-Ḥākim said, "One of the pillars of ḥadīth from whom Muslim narrated a great deal concerning fundamental principles and also as confirmatory material for other ḥadīth. Mālik narrated from him, and he [Mālik] is the judge concerning the shaykhs of Madīnah, the discriminatory person who can discriminate gold from false gold. Ibn Qāniᶜ dated his death as 138 AH. His father was Abū Ṣāliḥ Dhakwān as-Sammān az-Ziyat the Madīnan.

Sulaymān ibn Abī Ḥathmah. Ibn Ḥibbān said, "He was a Companion and one of the eminent Muslims and their people of right action. ᶜUmar put him in charge of the market, and made people follow him as imām in the standing [in *tarāwīḥ*] in Ramaḍān, as az-Zurqānī mentioned."

Sulaymān ibn Yasār is one of the notables. An-Nasā᾽ī said, "He was one of the imāms." Abū Zurᶜah said, "An eminent and trusted trustworthy narrator." He died in 107 AH. That is how it is in *Isᶜāf al-mubaṭṭa᾽* of as-Suyūṭī. Az-Zuhri said, "He was one of the ᶜulamā᾽." Az-Zuhri said, "He was a well trusted and trustworthy narrator. He died in 107 AH."

Summayy [ḥadīth 976] the mawlā of Abū Bakr ibn ᶜAbd ar-Raḥmān ibn al-Ḥārith ibn Hishām.

Suwayd ibn Nuᶜmān ibn Mālik ibn ᶜĀ᾽id ibn Majdaᶜah ibn Ḥashm ibn Ḥārithah al-Anṣārī al-Awsī. He was present at the [pledge of] Riḍwān, and some say at Uḥud and the events after it. He is counted as one of the people of Madīnah and his ḥadīth are counted as theirs. That is how it is in *Jāmiᶜ al-uṣūl*.

T

At-Tawʾamah is Bint Umayyah ibn Khalf the Madīnan, the sister of Rabīʿah ibn Umayyah ibn Khalf. She had a twin sister in the womb and so for that reason she is called at-Tawʾamah (the twin), and Ṣāliḥ Nabhān al-Madīnī is ascribed to her. That is what Abū Saʿd as-Samʿānī said in the book *al-Ansāb*.

Ṭalḥah ibn ʿAbd al-Mālik al-Aylī. Abū Dāwūd, an-Nasāʾī and a group regarded him as a trustworthy narrator, as is in *Isʿāf al-mubaṭṭaʾ* of as-Suyūṭī.

Ṭalḥah ibn ʿAbdullāh ibn ʿAwf was the nephew of ʿAbd ar-Raḥmān ibn ʿAwf and he was a trustworthy narrator who narrated a great deal, and a faqīh and Follower. He died in 97 AH.

Ṭalḥah ibn ʿAmr ibn ʿUthmān al-Ḥaḍramī the Makkan is spoken about [critically]. He said in *Tahdhīb at-tahdhīb*, "He narrated from ʿAṭāʾ ibn Abī Rabāḥ, Muḥammad ibn ʿAmr ibn ʿAlqamah, Ibn az-Zubayr, Saʿīd ibn Jubayr and others. Those who narrated from him include Jarīr ibn Ḥāzim, ath-Thawrī, Abū Dāwūd aṭ-Ṭayālisī, Wakīʿ and others. Aḥmad said, 'Nothing, and his ḥadīth are to be abandoned.' Ibn Maʿīn said, 'He is nothing, weak.' Al-Jūzajānī said, 'Unacceptable in his ḥadīth, but Ibn ʿAdī narrated some of his ḥadīth.' He said, 'Trustworthy people narrated from him but in people in general of what he narrates he is not followed.' ʿAbd ar-Razzāq said, 'I heard Muʿammar saying, "I, Shuʿbah, ath-Thawrī and Ibn Jarīr gathered together and a shaykh came to us and dictated four thousand ḥadīth to us from memory, without making a mistake except in two places while we were looking at the book. The mistake was not from us nor from him, but it was only from a higher narrator. The man was Ṭalḥah ibn ʿAmr.'" (Abridged) This weakness does not harm him in the basic matter intended, because ʿIkrimah ibn ʿAmmār followed him in his narration from ʿAṭāʾ, and Saʿīd ibn Jubayr followed ʿAṭāʾ in the narration of aṭ-Ṭaḥāwī.

Ṭalḥah ibn ᶜUbaydullāh was one of the ten given the good news [of the Garden]. He was Ṭalḥah ibn ᶜUbaydullāh ibn ᶜUthmān ibn ᶜAmr of Quraysh and Taym. He was one of the first forerunners who were present at Uḥud and everything after it. It is narrated of him that he said, "The Messenger of Allah ﷺ named me on the day of Uḥud, Ṭalḥah al-Khayr [the good], and on the day of Difficulty, Ṭalḥah al-Fayyāḍ [the overflowing], and on the day of Ḥunayn Ṭalḥah al-Jawwādd [the liberally generous]." He was a shahīd in the battle of the Camel in 36 AH, and has many virtues which Ibn al-Athīr mentioned in *Asad al-ghābah fī maᶜrifat aṣ-ṣaḥābah.*

Ṭāwūs was Ibn Kaysān al-Yamānī, and some say that his name was Dhakwān and that Ṭāwūs (Peacock) was his honorific. He was a Follower who was a trustworthy narrator, and he died in 106 AH, but some say after that, as az-Zurqānī mentioned.

Thābit ibn Ḍaḥḥāk ibn Khalīfah al-Anṣārī al-Ashbīlī is the well known Companion. He died in 64 AH according to the correct position, as is in *al-Iṣābah* and elsewhere.

Thābit ibn Qays ibn Shammās al-Anṣārī was one of the notables of the Anṣār who was present at Uḥud and those battles after it. He was the Imām Khaṭīb [who gave the khuṭbah] of the Anṣār, and was a shahīd on the Day of al-Yamāmah in 12 AH, as is in *Jāmiᶜ al-uṣūl.*

Thaᶜlabah ibn Abī Mālik al-Quraẓī. There is disagreement as to whether or not he was a Companion. Ibn Maᶜīn said, "He saw [the Prophet ﷺ]." Ibn Saᶜd said, "His father – Abū Mālik whose name was ᶜAbdullāh ibn Sām – came from the Yemen and he was from [the tribe of] Kindah. He married a woman of Qurayẓah and was known as [al-Quraẓī because of] them," as az-Zurqānī mentioned.

Thawr ibn Yazīd ibn Ziyād al-Kilāᶜī – and it is said he was ar-Rajabī – Abū Khālid al-Ḥimṣī. He narrated from Makḥūl, Rajā᾽ ibn Ḥaywah, ᶜAṭā᾽, ᶜIkrimah and others, and from him narrated the two Sufyāns, Mālik and others. Ibn Saᶜd, Aḥmad ibn Ṣāliḥ, Duḥaym, Yaḥyā ibn Saᶜīd, Wakīᶜ and others regarded him as a trustworthy narrator. He died in 55 AH, as is in *Tahdhīb at-tahdhīb*.

Thawr ibn Zayd ad-Dīlī – their mawlā – the Madīnan. Ibn Maᶜīn, Abū Zurᶜah and an-Nasāʾī regarded him as a trustworthy narrator. He died in 135 AH, as is in *Isᶜāf al-mubaṭṭaʾ* of as-Suyūṭī.

Aṭ-Ṭufayl ibn Ubayy ibn Kaᶜb al-Anṣārī al-Khazrajī was one of the trustworthy narrators of the Followers. It is said that he was born in the time of the Prophet ﷺ, and that his ḥadīth are precious. His kunyā was Abū Baṭn as Ibn al-Athīr mentioned in *Jāmiᶜ al-uṣūl*.

U

ᶜUbādah ibn aṣ-Ṣāmit is Abu'l-Walīd al-Anṣārī al-Khazrajī, one of the chiefs who was present at both of [the pledges of allegiances at] al-ᶜAqabah, and who was present at Badr, Uḥud, the pledge of allegiance called Riḍwān, and all of the major events and battles. He died in Shām in the khilāfah of Muᶜāwiyah, as is in *al-Iṣābah* and elsewhere.

ᶜUbādah ibn Tamīm from his uncle ᶜUtbah. This is found in many copies [in ḥadīth 970], but what is in the *Muwaṭṭa᾽* of Yaḥyā is "Mālik from ᶜAbbād ibn Tamīm al-Māzinī [see his entry] from his paternal uncle..." and this is how al-Bukhārī narrated it in the chapters on mosques, the chapters on clothing, and the chapters on seeking permission to enter, and Muslim in the chapters on clothing, Abū Dāwūd in [the chapters on] courtesy, at-Tirmidhī in seeking permission, and he said that it is good and ṣaḥīḥ, and an-Nasā᾽ī in *ṣalāh*, all of them by way of Mālik. At-Tirmidhī stated that the paternal uncle of ᶜAbbād ibn Tamīm al-Māzinī was ᶜAbdullāh ibn Zayd al-Māzinī [see his entry], as do the commentators of *Ṣaḥīḥ al-Bukhārī*, Ibn Ḥajar in *Fatḥ al-Bārī*, al-ᶜAynī in *ᶜUmdat al-aārī*, al-Kirmānī in *al-Kawākib ad-darārī*, and al-Qasṭallānīī in *Irshād as-sārī*. They also mention that ᶜAbbād is spelt thus, and ᶜAbdullāh ibn Zayd his paternal uncle is the brother of his mother's father, and we have previously mentioned both of them.

ᶜUbayd [in ḥadīth 28] is probably the father of Ḥabīb or someone else. There are in the book *Thiqāt at-tābiᶜīn* by Ibn Ḥibbān many Kūfans and people of Shām whose names were ᶜUbayd, but to this day I don't know specifically who he is, and perhaps Allah will uncover some new information for me. This [Ḥabīb narrating from ᶜUbayd] is what we have found in some copies but I do not think it is sound, and I think what is sound is that which is in some dependable copies that it is from Ḥabīb ibn ᶜUbayd, so that the narrator from Abu'd-Dardā᾽ is Ḥabīb without any intermediary.

U

ᶜUbayd ibn Fayrūz. As-Suyūṭī mentions that he was Abu'ḍ-Ḍaḥḥāk the Kūfan whom an-Nasāʾī and Abū Ḥātim considered a trustworthy narrator. Ibn ᶜAbd al-Barr said, "The narrators from Mālik do not differ over this ḥadīth [632]. Only ᶜAmr narrates from Sulaymān ibn ᶜAbd ar-Raḥmān who narrates it from ᶜUbayd leaving out Mālik's mention of Sulaymān. The ḥadīth is unknown except from him, and no one other than him narrated it from ᶜUbayd, and ᶜUbayd himself is only known for this ḥadīth. A large group narrated from Sulaymān among whom were Shuᶜbah, al-Layth from ᶜAmr."

ᶜUbayd ibn Jurayj at-Taymī – their mawlā – the Madīnan, was one of the trustworthy narrators of the Followers, as al-Ḥāfiẓ ibn Ḥajar mentions.

ᶜUbaydullāh ibn ᶜAbdullāh ibn ᶜUmar was one of the notable Followers. He was a firmly established and trustworthy narrator. He died before his brother Sālim, as Ibn al-Athīr said.

ᶜUbaydullāh ibn ᶜAbdullāh ibn ᶜUtbah ibn Masᶜūd al-Hudhalī Abū ᶜAbdullāh was one of the seven fuqahāʾ of Madīnah. He narrated from his father, Ibn ᶜAbbās, Ibn ᶜUmar and an-Nuᶜmān ibn Bashīr. From him narrated az-Zuhrī, Sālim Abu'n-Naḍr and a party of others. Abū Zurᶜah, al-ᶜIjlī and more than one regarded him as a trustworthy narrator. He died in 94 AH or 95 AH, but some say 98 AH. That is how it is in *Isᶜāf al-mubaṭṭaʾ bi rijāl al-Muwaṭṭaʾ*".

ᶜUbaydullāh ibn ᶜUmar ibn Ḥafṣ ibn ᶜĀṣim ibn Amīr al-Muʾminīn ᶜUmar ibn al-Khattāb Abū ᶜUthmān al-ᶜUmarī al-ᶜAdawī the Madīnan. He is one of the greatest of the trustworthy narrators. He narrated one ḥadīth from Umm Khālid bint Khālid the Companion and from al-Qāsim ibn Muḥammad ibn Abī Bakr aṣ-Ṣiddīq, Sālim ibn ᶜAbdullāh ibn ᶜUmar, ᶜAṭāʾ, Nāfiᶜ, al-Maqburī, az-Zuhrī and others. From him narrated Shuᶜbah, the two Sufyāns, Yaḥyā al-Qaṭṭān and others. An-Nasāʾī said he was a reliable trustworthy narrator. Abū Ḥātim said, "I asked Aḥmad about ᶜUbaydullāh, Mālik and Ayyūb, as to which of them was more firmly established in narrating from Nāfiᶜ? and he said, "ᶜUbaydullāh is the one of them who memorised best and the most firmly established of them, and the one who narrated most.'" Aḥmad ibn Ṣāliḥ said, "ᶜUbaydullāh is preferrable to me to Mālik [in narrating] from Nāfiᶜ." He died in 147 AH in Madīnah. That is how adh-Dhahabī mentioned it in *Tadhkirat al-ḥuffāẓ*.

ᶜUbaydullāh al-Khawlānī was the foster son of Maymūnah and a trustworthy narrator. The two Shaykhs narrate from him as is mentioned by az-Zurqānī .

Ubayy ibn Kaᶜb ibn Qays al-Anṣārī an-Najjārī Abu'l-Mundhir. He was one of the eminent Companions and the chief of the Qurʾān reciters. He died in 29 AH or 32 AH, and people say other things [dates], as is in *at-Taqrīb*.

ᶜUmar ibn ᶜAbd al-ᶜAzīz was one of the Khulafāʾ ar-Rāshidūn. He was Abū Ḥafṣ ᶜUmar ibn ᶜAbd al-ᶜAzīz ibn Marwān ibn al-Ḥakam al-Umawī of Quraysh. He had such knowledge, doing without the world [*zuhd*], taqwā, justice, abstinence, and good character that there was no one like him in the days of his amirate. He was appointed khalīfah after Sulaymān ibn ᶜAbd al-Mālik ibn Marwān in 99 AH, and he died in 101 AH. He had numerous virtues, and is counted as one of the renewers of the dīn at the beginning of a century, as is in *Jāmiᶜ al-uṣūl*.

ᶜUmar ibn ᶜAbdullāh ibn Kaᶜb as-Salamī [ḥadīth 877]. Thus it is in the copy on which al-Qārī and others wrote commentary but in the *Muwaṭṭaʾ* of Yaḥyā it is ᶜAmr. As-Suyūṭī said in *al-Isᶜāf*, "ᶜAmr ibn ᶜAbdullāh ibn Kaᶜb ibn Mālik al-Anṣārī as-Salamī narrated from Nāfiᶜ ibn Jubayr, and Yazīd ibn Khuṣayfah narrated from him. An-Nasāʾī regarded him as a trustworthy narrator."

ᶜUmar ibn Dharr al-Hamdānī. Dharr is spelt out thus by al-Fattanī in *al-Mughnī* and not Dhirr as al-Qārī mentioned. He was ibn ᶜAbdullāh ibn Zurārah al-Hamdānī by ascription to Hamdān a tribe which resided in Kūfa. As-Samᶜānī said, "One of the people of Kūfa. He narrated from ᶜAṭāʾ and Mujāhid, and Wakīᶜ and the people of ᶜIrāq narrated from him. He died in 150 AH. Ibn Ḥibbān said he was one of the Murjiʾah." There is in *at-Taqrīb*, "ᶜUmar ibn Dharr ibn ᶜAbdullāh ibn Zurārah al-Hamdānī al-Murhabī [the monastic] the Kūfan, Abū Dharr the trustworthy narrator who was accused of being one of the Murjiʾah."

ᶜUmar ibn Ḥusayn was a trustworthy narrator from whom Muslim and at-Tirmidhī narrated. He was ᶜUmar ibn Ḥusayn ibn ᶜAbdullāh al-Jumaḥī – their mawlā – Abū Qudāmah al-Makkī, as is in *at-Taqrīb*.

ᶜUmar ibn al-Khattāb is Abū Ḥafṣ ᶜUmar ibn al-Khattāb al-ᶜAdawī of Quraysh. He is one of "the ten" [promised the Garden], and one of the Khulafāʾ ar-Rāshidūn. He was named al-Fārūq. He accepted Islam in the sixth year of prophethood, but some say the fifth year. Islam became public with his Islam. Ibn Masᶜūd said, "By Allah! I reckon that if the knowledge of ᶜUmar was put into one pan of the scales and the knowledge of all other people on the earth were to be put into another pan, the knowledge of ᶜUmar would be heavier." He has many merits, and was killed as a shahīd in Dhu'l-Ḥijjah 23 AH. From *Asmāʾ rijāl al-mishkāh* by the author of the *Mishkāh*.

ᶜUmar ibn ᶜUthmān ibn ᶜAffān. Ibn ᶜAbd al-Barr said, "Thus Mālik said, but all the other companions of Ibn Shihāb say ᶜAmr ibn ᶜUthmān and Ibn Bukayr narrated it from Mālik with some doubt and said, 'From ᶜUmar ibn ᶜUthmān or ᶜAmr ibn ᶜUthmān.' Ibn al-Qāsim said about him, 'From ᶜAmr ibn ᶜUthmān.' But what is established from Mālik was that he was ᶜUmar, as Yaḥyā and all the other narrators narrated it. There is no disagreement that ᶜUthmān had a son called ᶜUmar and another called ᶜAmr, but the only disagreement is concerning whether this ḥadīth is from ᶜUmar or ᶜAmr. The companions of Ibn Shihāb apart from Mālik say that he is ᶜAmr ibn ᶜUthmān and Mālik says that he is ᶜUmar, and ash-Shāfiᶜī and Yaḥyā ibn Saᶜīd al-Qaṭṭān acquainted him with that and he refused to retract and said that he is ᶜUmar. The truth is that Mālik is the one against whom others have to be measured in terms of memorisation and exact attention to detail, but no one is safe from making mistakes and the people of ḥadīth refuse anyone else in this chain of transmission than ᶜAmr." Al-ᶜIrāqī said, "It does not necessarily follow from the fact that Mālik alone among the trustworthy narrators narrates the name of this narrator thus, along with the fact that each of them is a trustworthy narrator, that the text [of the ḥadīth] should be rejected nor that it should be regarded as an extremely rare and divergent text, for on the contrary it is in any case sound, and the most extreme case is that this chain of transmission [of the ḥadīth] would be regarded as rejected or extremely rare and divergent because of trustworthy narrators' differing with Mālik about that."

ᶜUmārah ibn Ṣayyād was ᶜUmārah ibn ᶜAbdullāh ibn Ṣayyād al-Anṣārī Abū Ayyūb the Madīnan, who was ascribed to his grandfather Ṣayyād. His father is the one about whom people said that he was the Dajjāl. Ibn Maᶜīn and an-Nasāʾī regarded him [ᶜUmārah] as a trustworthy narrator. He died after 130 AH, as is in *Isᶜāf al-mubaṭṭaʾ* of as-Suyūṭī.

Umaymah bint Ruqayqah. Ruqayqah was the sister of Khadījah, the mother of the muʾminīn, bint Khuwaylid ibn Asad so that Khadījah was Umaymah's maternal aunt. Her father was Najād ibn ᶜAbdullāh ibn ᶜUmayr, but some say ᶜAbdullāh ibn Najād of Quraysh, as is in *al-Istīᶜāb* and elsewhere.

ᶜUmayr the mawlā of Ibn ᶜAbbās was Ibn ᶜAbdullāh al-Hilālī. An-Nasāʾī and Ibn Ḥibbān regarded him as a trustworthy narrator. He died in 104 AH, as is in *al-Isᶜāf*.

ᶜUmayr ibn Saᶜd, but some say [ᶜUmayr ibn] Saᶜīd an-Nakhaᶜī aṣ-Ṣuhbānī by ascription to Ṣuhbān a clan of an-Nakhaᶜ. His kunyā was Abū Yaḥyā. He was a reliable and trustworthy narrator. He died in 107 AH but some say 115 AH. Thus it is in *al-Ansāb* and *at-Taqrīb*.

Umm Bujayd is best known by her kunyā, and her name was Ḥawwāʾ bint Yazīd ibn as-Sakan.

Umm al-Faḍl was Lubābah bint al-Ḥārith al-Hilāliyyah, the sister of Maymūnah the mother of the muʾminūn, and the wife of al-ᶜAbbās ibn ᶜAbd al-Muṭṭalib. It is said that she was the first woman to accept Islam after Khadījah, as is in *al-Istīᶜāb*.

Umm Ḥabībah the wife of the Prophet ﷺ and the daughter of Abū Sufyān. Her name was Ramlah, and there is no disagreement about that except from a few solitary individuals. She died in 44 AH, as is in *Isᶜāf al-mubaṭṭaʾ* of as-Suyūṭī.

Umm Hāniʾ was the full sister [*shaqīqah*] of ᶜAlī, and their mother was Fāṭimah bint Asad, also the mother of Ṭālib, ᶜAqīl and Jaᶜfar. There is disagreement about her name, and some say Hind and some say Fākhitah. She was married to Hubayrah ibn Abī Wahb ibn ᶜAmr ibn ᶜĀʾidh ibn ᶜImrān ibn Makhzūm, and accepted Islam in the year of the Opening [of Makkah to Islam]. That is how it is in *al-Istīᶜāb*.

Umm Kulthūm bint Abī Bakr was a Follower. Her father, Abū Bakr ﷺ died while she was yet unborn and she was born after his death. She narrated a ḥadīth as a mursal ḥadīth because of which Ibn Mandah and Ibn as-Sakan mentioned her among the Companions, but they made a mistake, as az-Zurqānī said.

Umm Qays is the sister of ᶜUkāshah. She became a Muslim very early on and emigrated to Madīnah. Her mawlā, ᶜAdī ibn Dīnār, narrated from her, as did Wābiṣah ibn Maᶜbad and others. That is how it is in *al-Isᶜāf*. Az-Zurqānī said her name was Judhāmah, but some say it was Āminah.

Umm Salamah is Hind bint Abī Umayyah, whose name [Abū Umayyah's] was Ḥudhayfah ibn al-Mughīrah ibn ᶜAbdullāh. She was of Quraysh and [the clan] Makhzūm. The Messenger of Allah ﷺ married her right after the battle of Badr. She died in Shawwāl 62 AH as is in *Isᶜāf al-mubaṭṭaʾ* of as-Suyūṭī. Before the Messenger of Allah ﷺ she was married to Abū Salamah ibn ᶜAbd to whom she bore ᶜUmar and Salamah, as is in *al-Istīᶜāb*.

Umm Sulaym is Bint Milḥān ibn Khālid ibn Zayd ibn Ḥarām ibn Jundub of an-Najjār and the Anṣār. There is disagreement about her name and some said Sahlah, Rumaylah, Mulaykah, or al-Ghumayḍāʾ. She was married to Mālik ibn an-Naḍr the father of Anas ibn Mālik before Islam and she bore him Anas. When she accepted Islam, it was offered to her husband who grew enraged and died there and then. After him Abū Ṭalḥah al-Anṣārī married her to whom she bore ᶜAbdullāh ibn Abī Ṭalḥah. That is how it is in *al-Istīᶜāb*. Mulaykah was the grandmother of Isḥāq ibn ᶜAbdullāh ibn Abī Ṭalḥah, Mālik says. The pronoun in "his grandmother" [ḥadīth 179] refers to Isḥāq and she was the mother of his father ᶜAbdullāh ibn Abī Ṭalḥah and is Umm Sulaym bint Milḥān wife of Abū Ṭalḥah al-Anṣārī. She was the mother of Anas ibn Mālik. She had been married to his father Mālik ibn an-Naḍr whom she bore Anas ibn Mālik and al-Barāʾ ibn Mālik, and then later Abū Ṭalḥah married her, as Ibn ᶜAbd al-Barr said. Her name was Sahlah or Rumaylah, Rumaythah, Mulaykah, al-Ghumayḍāʾ or ar-Rumayṣāʾ (an eminent woman Companion who died during the khilāfah of ᶜUthmān, *Taqrīb at-tahdhīb* 2/622). She had been married to Mālik ibn Abi'n-Naḍr, the father of Anas, before Islam. When Allah brought Islam she accepted it along with her people, but when she offered it to her husband he grew enraged and died as a kāfir. Abū Ṭalḥah married her and she bore him a son who died in infancy, the aforementioned Abū ᶜUmayr in the ḥadīth of an-Nughayr. Then she bore him ᶜAbdullāh ibn Abī Ṭalḥah in whom he received blessing and who is the father of Isḥāq, who had ten brothers from each of whom knowledge was taken, as Ibn ᶜAbd al-Barr mentioned in *al-Istiᶜāb.* She was al-Ghumayṣāʾ, but some say ar-Rumayṣāʾ, Sahlah, Unayfā, Rumaythah, or Rumaylah. Her mother was Mulaykah bint Mālik, as is in *at-Tanwīr* (169 S). The Ḥāfiẓ said that she was Mulaykah.

Umm Sulaymān see ash-Shifāʾ.

An Umm Walad of Ibrāhīm ibn ᶜAbd ar-Raḥmān ibn ᶜAwf. The author of *al-Azhār* and *al-Ghawāmiḍ* transmitted that her name was Ḥamīdah. Az-Zurqānī said, "She was an acceptable but younger Follower." Ḥāfiẓ mentioned in *at-Taqrīb*, "Ḥamīdah [narrated] from Umm Salamah. It is said that she is the Umm Walad of Ibrāhīm. She is acceptable, of the fourth [generation]."

ᶜUrwah ibn Udhaynah. [ᶜUrwah's father's name] Udhaynah was an honorific and his name was Yaḥyā ibn Mālik ibn al-Ḥārith ibn ᶜAmr al-Laythī. ᶜUrwah was a poet of good love poetry. He was a trustworthy narrator, but he has only this one ḥadīth in the *Muwaṭṭa*ᵓ. His grandfather Mālik ibn al-Ḥārith has a narration from ᶜAlī, as Ibn ᶜAbd al-Barr and others mention.

ᶜUrwah ibn az-Zubayr ibn al-ᶜAwwām al-Asadī Abū ᶜAbdullāh the Madīnan. Ibn ᶜUyaynah said, "There are three people who had the most knowledge of ᶜĀᵓishah's ḥadīth: al-Qāsim, ᶜUrwah and ᶜAmrah bint ᶜAbd ar-Raḥmān." He narrated from his father and from his brother ᶜAbdullāh, and from ᶜAlī and his two sons, and ᶜĀᵓishah. From him narrated his sons ᶜAbdullāh, Muḥammad, ᶜUthmān and Hishām. He died in 94 AH. That is how it is in *Isᶜāf al-mubaṭṭa*ᵓ of as-Suyūṭī.

Usāmah the son of Zayd ibn Ḥārithah ibn Sharāḥīl al-Hāshimī the mawlā of the Messenger of Allah ﷺ. He had many virtues. The Prophet ﷺ said to ᶜĀᵓishah, "Love him because I love him," which at-Tirmidhī narrated. He appointed him the amīr of the army among whom were ᶜUmar, and he himself tied the standard for him. He died in Madīnah or in the surrounding countryside of the villages in 54 AH, and some say other things, as an-Nawawī mentioned in *Tahdhīb al-asmā*ᵓ *wa'l-lughāt*

Usāmah ibn Zayd the Madīnan. Adh-Dhahabī said in *Mīzān al-iᶜtidāl*, "Usāmah ibn Zayd al-Laythī – their mawlā – the Madīnan, who [narrated] from Ṭāwūs and his generation. From him narrated Ibn Wahb, Zayd ibn al-Ḥubbāb, ᶜUbaydullāh ibn Mūsā. Aḥmad said, 'He is not anything,' upon which his son elaborated, saying, 'If you examine his ḥadīth, you will recognise things which are not acceptable.' Yaḥyā ibn Maᶜīn said he was a trustworthy narrator, but Yaḥyā al-Qaṭṭān used to regard him as weak. An-Nasāʾī said, 'He is not strong.' Ibn ᶜAdī said, 'There is no harm in him.' ᶜAbbās and Aḥmad ibn Abī Maryam narrated from Yaḥyā, 'A trustworthy narrator.' Ibn Abī Maryam added from him, 'A decisive proof.' Abū Ḥātim said, 'His ḥadīth are to be written down, but he is not to be used as a decisive proof.' He died in 153 AH." (Abridged) There is in *at-Taqrīb*, "He was an utterly truthful man who made mistakes." He has a long biographical notice in *Tahdhīb at-tahdhīb.*

ᶜUthmān ibn Abi'l-ᶜĀṣ. The Prophet ﷺ appointed him as governor of Ṭāʾif, and then later Abū Bakr and ᶜUmar both made him the amīr. He died in 51 AH, which is mentioned in *Asad al-ghābah fī maᶜrifat aṣ-ṣaḥābah* and elsewhere.

ᶜUthmān ibn ᶜAffān ibn Abi'l-ᶜĀṣ ibn Umayyah ibn ᶜAbd Shams ibn ᶜAbd Manāf al-Qurashī, Dhu'n-Nurayn – the Possessor of the Two Lights. He has a great quantity of virtues and was killed as a shahīd in Dhu'l-Ḥijjah 35 AH as it is in *at-Taqrīb* and *Jāmiᶜ al-uṣūl*. In *Isᶜāf al-mubaṭṭaʾ* of as-Suyūṭī it is said that he was killed on Jumuᶜah the 18th of Dhu'l-Ḥijjah 35 AH.

ᶜUthmān ibn Isḥāq ibn Kharashah was one of the Followers whom Ibn Maᶜīn regarded as a trustworthy narrator. He was of Quraysh and of [Banī] ᶜĀmir and a Madīnan, as is in *at-Taqrīb.*

ᶜUwaymir ibn Ashqar ibn ᶜAwf al-Anṣārī. Some said he was Ibn Ashqar ibn ᶜAdī ibn Khansāʾ ibn Mabdhūl ibn ᶜAmr ibn Ghanam ibn Māzin ibn an-Najjār al-Anṣārī al-Māzinī. He was present at Badr, and ᶜAbbād ibn Tamīm al-Māzinī narrated from him as a mursal ḥadīth, as Ibn al-Athīr said in *Jāmiᶜ al-uṣūl.*

W

Wahb ibn Kaysān. He said in *al-Isᶜāf,* "Wahb ibn Kaysān of Quraysh their mawlā, Abū Nuᶜaym the Madīnan. An-Nasāʾī and Ibn Saᶜd regarded him as a trustworthy narrator. He died in 127 AH."

Wāʾil al-Ḥaḍramī by ascription to Ḥaḍramawt a land in the Yemen. Wāʾil ibn Ḥujr was a great king there. When news of the appearance of the Prophet ﷺ reached him he left his kingdom and set off to go to him. The Prophet ﷺ gave people the news of his arrival three days before he came, and when he came he drew him near to where he sat and said, "This is Wāʾil who has come to you from the land of the Yemen – a remote land – [and he has come] obediently without coercion desiring Allah and His Messenger. O Allah bless Wāʾil and his children." Then he granted him some land. He died during the amirate of Muᶜāwiyah. His sons narrated from him: ᶜAlqamah and ᶜAbd al-Jabbār. That is how it is in the *Ansāb as-Samᶜānī.* In the *Jāmiᶜ al-uṣūl* by Ibn al-Athīr there is, "Abū Hunaydah Wāʾil ibn Ḥujr ibn Rabīᶜah ibn Wāʾil al-Ḥaḍramī was one of the princes and chiefs of Ḥaḍramawt and his father had been one of their kings. He came as a delegate to the Prophet ﷺ and accepted Islam, and he ﷺ gave people the news of his coming [beforehand]."

Al-Walīd ibn ᶜAbdullāh ibn Ṣayyād. He was the brother of ᶜAmārah ibn ᶜAbdullāh ibn Ṣayyād. Az-Zurqānī said, "Al-Bukhārī did not mention him in his *Tārīkh,* nor did Abū Ḥātim, and Ibn ᶜAbd al-Barr didn't write a biographical notice for him, but Ibn Ḥibbān mentioned him in *ath-Thiqāt,* and Mālik's narration from him is sufficient evidence of his trustworthiness."

Wāqid ibn Saᶜd ibn Muᶜādh al-Anṣārī was a trustworthy narrator from whom Muslim and the three transmitted. He died in 120 AH, as az-Zurqānī mentioned. Ibn ᶜAbd al-Barr said, "All the other narrators say 'from Wāqid ibn ᶜAmr ibn Saᶜd ibn Muᶜādh.'"

Wāsiᶜ ibn Ḥabbān ibn Munqidh ibn ᶜAmr al-Anṣārī. Abū Zurᶜah regarded him as a trustworthy narrator, as is in *Isᶜāf al-mubaṭṭaʾ* of as-Suyūṭī.

The wife of ᶜAbdullāh ibn Masᶜūd from the tribe of Thaqīf [ḥadīth 789]. Her name was Zaynab bint ᶜAbdullāh ibn Muᶜāwiyah ibn ᶜAttāb ibn al-Asᶜad ibn Ghāḍirah. She was a Companion who narrated from the Prophet ﷺ and from her husband. The son of her brother and Busr ibn Saᶜīd narrated from her, as is in *al-Istīᶜāb* by Ibn ᶜAbd al-Barr.

Y

Yaḥyā ibn al-Jazzār [son of the butcher]. He said in *at-Taqrīb* and *al-Kāshif,* "Yaḥyā ibn al-Jazzār al-ᶜUranī the Kūfan. It is said that the name of his father was Zabān. He narrated from ᶜAlī and ᶜĀʾishah, and from him narrated al-Ḥakam and al-Ḥasan al-ᶜUranī. He was a trustworthy narrator who was utterly truthful, but who was accused of being a fanatical Shīᶜah."

Yaḥyā ibn Muḥammad ibn Ṭaḥlāʾ was Madīnan from the tribe of Taym. He narrated from his father and ᶜUthmān. Mālik, ad-Darāwardī and others narrated from him. Ibn Ḥibbān mentions him among the trustworthy Followers. That is how az-Zurqānī mentions him. His father was ᶜAbd ar-Raḥmān ibn ᶜUthmān ibn ᶜUbaydullāh at-Taymī the Madīnan, and he was one of the Companions. He was killed along with Ibn az-Zubayr. His son ᶜUthmān, who was of the fifth generation, is trustworthy. That is how it is in *at-Taqrīb*.

Yaḥyā ibn Saᶜīd is the Shaykh al-Islām Abū Saᶜīd Yaḥyā ibn Saᶜīd ibn Qays ibn ᶜAmr al-Anṣārī the Madīnan the qāḍī of Madīnah. He narrated from Anas, ᶜAdī ibn Thābit, as-Sāʾib ibn Yazīd, Abū Umāmah, Saᶜīd ibn al-Musayyab, al-Qāsim ibn Muḥammad, ᶜAlī ibn al-Ḥusayn and others. From him narrated Abū Ḥanīfah, Shuᶜbah, Mālik, the two Sufyāns, the two Ḥammāds, Ibn al-Mubārak and a great number of other people. Ayyūb as-Sakhtiyānī said, "I left no one behind in Madīnah with more fiqh than him." Yaḥyā al-Qaṭṭān said, "He has precedence over az-Zuhrī." Abū Ḥātim said, "He is a trustworthy narrator, the equal of az-Zuhrī." Al-ᶜIjlī said, "An eminent faqīh and trustworthy narrator." He died in al-Hāshimiyyah in 143 AH. That is how it is in *Tadhkirat al-ḥuffāẓ* by adh-Dhahabī. Ibn Saᶜd said, "He was a trustworthy narrator who had many ḥadīth, and he is a firmly established proof." He died in 143 AH. That is how it is in *Isᶜāf al-mubaṭṭaʾ* of as-Suyūṭī.

Yaᶜqūb ibn Ibrāhīm is the Imām Abū Yūsuf the qāḍī and companion of Imām Abū Ḥanīfah. Adh-Dhahabī said in *Tadhkirat al-ḥuffāẓ*, "Qāḍī

Abū Yūsuf, the faqīh of the ʿIrāqiss, Yaʿqūb ibn Ibrāhīm al-Anṣārī the Kūfan was the companion of Abū Ḥanīfah. He heard Hishām ibn ʿUrwah, Abū Isḥāq ash-Shaybānī, ʿAṭā' ibn as-Sā'ib and people of their generation. From him narrated Muḥammad ibn al-Ḥasan the faqīh, Aḥmad ibn Ḥanbal, Bishr ibn al-Walīd and Yaḥyā ibn Maʿīn. He grew up in the search for knowledge, but his father was a poor man and Abū Ḥanīfah paid frequent attention to him [probably maintaining him]. Al-Muznī said, 'Of all the people he is the one who most follows ḥadīth.' Yaḥyā ibn Maʿīn said, 'There is no one among the people of theory (*ra'y*) who has more ḥadīth and is more firmly established than Abū Yūsuf.' Aḥmad said, 'He was fair and just in ḥadīth.' He died in Rabīʿ al-Ākhir 182 AH when he was 69 years old. There are many stories about him in knowledge and in leadership, and I have dedicated a volume to him and a volume to his companion Muḥammad ibn al-Ḥasan. His oldest shaykh was Ḥuṣayn ibn ʿAbd ar-Raḥmān." Abridged. He has a long biographical notice in *Ansāb as-Samʿānī* which I have mentioned in the introduction to this commentary just as I have also mentioned his biography in the *Muqaddimat al-Hidāyah* and in *an-Nāfiʿ al-kabīr liman yuṭāliʿu al-jāmiʿ aṣ-ṣaghīr* and in *al-Fawā'id al-bahiyyah fī tarājim al-ḥanafiyyah.*

Yaʿqūb ibn Zayd ibn Ṭalḥah of Quraysh and of Taym was an utterly truthful person and a Madīnan. His father Zayd [mistakenly written "Abū Zayd"] ibn Ṭalḥah was a minor Follower. Al-Ḥākim thought that he was a Companion, but it is not like that, as al-Ḥāfiẓ expanded upon in *al-Iṣābah*. His grandfather was ʿAbdullāh [an addition here is "ibn ʿUbaydullāh" which seems to be mistaken] ibn Abī Mulaykah, and it is said that his name [Abū Mulaykah's] was Zuhayr at-Taymī the Madīnan, a trustworthy narrator of the Followers. He died in 117 AH, as az-Zurqānī said.

Yaʿqūb the Madīnan and mawlā of al-Ḥuraqah is acceptable. His son was ʿAbd ar-Raḥmān al-Ḥuraqī – by ascription to Ḥuraqah, a clan of Hamdān, but some say of Juhaynah, which is the correct position. ʿAbd ar-Rahman's son was Abū Shibl al-ʿAlā' the mawlā of al-Ḥuruqah who died in 132 AH. Ibn Ḥibbān mentioned both of them in *ath-Thiqāt* as is in *at-Taqrīb* and *al-Ansāb*.

Yarfā' the door-keeper or chamberlain of ᶜUmar had lived in the Jāhiliyyah, and he performed the Ḥajj with ᶜUmar in the khilāfah of Abū Bakr. He is mentioned in the two ṣaḥīḥ books concerning the story of the quarrel between ᶜAlī and ᶜAbbās over the ṣadaqah of the Messenger of Allah ﷺ as az-Zurqānī said.

Yasār ibn Numayr. Al-Ḥāfiẓ said in *at-Taqrīb,* "Yasār ibn Numayr the Madīnan was the mawlā of ᶜUmar ibn al-Khattāb. He was a trustworthy narrator and went to live in Kūfa."

Yazīd ibn ᶜAbdullāh ibn Qusayṭ. He said in *at-Taqrīb,* "Yazīd ibn ᶜAbdullāh ibn Qusayṭ ibn Usāmah al-Laythī Abū ᶜAbdullāh the Madīnan al-Aᶜraj is a trustworthy narrator. He died in 122 AH."

Yazīd ibn ᶜAbdullāh ibn Usāmah ibn al-Hād al-Laythī the Madīnan. Ibn Maᶜīn and an-Nasā'ī regarded him as a trustworthy narrator. He died in 139 AH, as is in *al-Isᶜāf.*

Yazīd ibn Jāriyah al-Anṣārī al-Awsī was the father of ᶜAbd ar-Raḥmān and Mujammiᶜ. Ibn Saᶜd mentions him as one of the Companions, and az-Zurqānī said the same. Ibn ᶜAbd al-Barr said in *al-Istīᶜāb,* "Yazīd ibn Ḥārithah (Ḥārithah and Jāriyah are identical if the letters are not marked with the diacriticals) al-Yarbūᶜī ibn ᶜĀmir ibn Mujammiᶜ ibn al-ᶜAṭāf, and he is Abū Mujammiᶜ."

Yazīd ibn Khuṣayfah was Yazīd ibn ᶜAbdullāh ibn Khuṣayfah ibn ᶜAbdullāh ibn Yazīd al-Kindī the Madīnan, and he was a trustworthy narrator from among the narrators used by everyone [of the major transmitters]. He is sometimes ascribed to his grandfather Khuṣayfah [as Ibn Khuṣayfah] as is mentioned in *at-Taqrīb* and others.

Yazīd ibn Nuᶜaym ibn Hazzāl was a minor Follower, as Ibn al-Athīr mentioned in *Asad al-ghābah fī maᶜrifat aṣ-ṣaḥābah* and *Jāmiᶜ al-uṣūl.*

Yazīd ibn Ṭalḥah ar-Rukānī – by ascription to Rukānah the father of Ṭalḥah – ibn ᶜAbd Yazīd ibn Hāshim. Ibn Ḥibbān mentioned this Yazīd in *Thiqāt at-tābiᶜīn* as is in *Sharḥ az-Zurqānī*.

Yazīd ibn Ziyād. Ibn Ḥajar said in *Taqrīb at-tahdhīb*, "Yazīd ibn Ziyād or ibn Abī Ziyād is probably ascribed to his grandfather [Ziyād], and is a mawlā of Banī Makhzūm and a Madīnan. He was trustworthy."

Yazīd ar-Raqāshī [ḥadīth 63 in which some have said that Saᶜīd ar-Raqāshī is a mistake for this Yazīd]. Adh-Dhahabī said in *al-Kāshif* in introducing him, "Yazīd ibn Abān ar-Raqāshī the worshipper narrated from Anas and al-Ḥasan, and from him narrated Ṣāliḥ al-Murrī and Ḥammād ibn Salamah, but he is weak." He mentioned in *Tahdhīb at-tahdhīb* in discussing ar-Rabīᶜ, "Yazīd ar-Raqāshī was one of his shaykhs," and in it there is no mention of [the name] Saᶜīd.

Yūnus ibn Abī Isḥāq as-Sabīᶜī. His kunyā was Abū Isrā'īl and he narrated from his father Abū Isḥāq. He died in 159 AH. There is in *at-Taqrīb*, "Yūnus ibn Abī Isḥāq as-Sabīᶜī Abū Isrā'īl the Kūfan was utterly truthful and made only a few mistakes. He died in 152 AH, according to the correct view."

Yūnus ibn Yūsuf ibn Ḥimās was one of the devotees of the People of Madīnah, and he was a trustworthy narrator. Ibn Ḥibbān said, "He is Yūsuf ibn Yūnus, and those who reverse the order [of these two names] have made a mistake," as is in *at-Taqrīb*.

Z

Az-Zabīr ibn ᶜAbd ar-Raḥmān ibn az-Zabīr ibn Bāṭiyā al-Quraẓī the Madīnan. The name in both cases is spelt Zabir according to all narrators of the *Muwaṭṭa*ᵓ except for Ibn Bakīr who narrated it as az-Zubayr in the first case and az-Zabīr in the second. Ibn ᶜAbd al-Barr said, "The correct position is that both are az-Zabīr, i.e. from Mālik." Ibn Ḥajar said in *al-Iṣābah,* "He is az-Zubayr as opposed to his grandfather who is az-Zabīr."

Zabrāᵓ, a mawlāh of Banī ᶜAdī ibn Kaᶜb. It is spelt thus according to Ibn al-Athīr.

Zayd Abū ᶜAyyāsh the mawlā of Banī Zuhrah. Abū Ḥanīfah regarded the ḥadīth [764] as defective because of him and he said, "It is based on Zayd Abū ᶜAyyāsh and he is unknown." Ibn Ḥazm said the same, but others replied that the ḥadīth is ṣaḥīḥ and that Zayd is not an unknown person. Az-Zurqānī said, "Zayd's kunyā was Abū ᶜAyyāsh and his father's name was ᶜAyyāsh and he was a Madīnan Follower who was utterly truthful. It is transmitted from Mālik that he was the mawlā of Saᶜd ibn Abī Waqqāṣ and some say that he was the mawlā of Banī Makhzūm." There is in the *Tahdhīb at-tahdhīb* by Ibn Ḥajar al-ᶜAsqalānī, "Zayd ibn ᶜAyyāsh Abū ᶜAyyāsh az-Zuraqī, but some say al-Makhzūmī. He narrated from Saᶜd, and from him narrated ᶜAbdullāh ibn Yazīd and ᶜImrān ibn Abī Unays. Ibn Ḥibbān mentioned him in *ath-Thiqāt,* and at-Tirmidhī, Ibn Khuzaymah and Ibn Ḥibbān declare the aforementioned ḥadīth [764] of his to be ṣaḥīḥ. Ad-Dāraquṭnī said he was a trustworthy narrator, and al-Ḥākim said in *al-Mustadrak,* 'This is a ṣaḥīḥ ḥadīth because of the unanimous agreement of the imāms of transmission on the imāmate of Mālik and that he is completely reliable in everything which he narrates since only the ṣaḥīḥ exists in his narrations, particularly as regards narration from the People of Madīnah. The two shaykhs did not narrate it since they feared the unknown character of Zayd.'" There is in *Fatḥ al-qadīr sharḥ al-Hidāyah,* "The author of *at-Tanqīḥ* said, 'There is no harm in Zayd ibn ᶜAyyāsh Abū ᶜAyyāsh az-Zuraqī the Madīnan. Our shaykhs mention from Abū Ḥanīfah that he is unknown, but his aspersion is refuted by saying that he is a trustworthy narrator and that Mālik narrated from him in the *Muwaṭṭaʾ*, and that he did not narrate from an unknown person. Al-Mundhirī said, 'How could he be unknown when two trustworthy narrators have narrated from him: ᶜAbdullāh ibn Yazīd and ᶜImrān ibn Abī Unays? They are both people whom Muslim used as proofs in his *Ṣaḥīḥ* and the imāms of this field recognise it. Mālik narrated his ḥadīth even though he took extraordinary precautions about his narrators.' Ibn al-Jawzī said in *at-Taḥqīq*, 'Abū Ḥanīfah said that he was unknown, but even if he did not know him the imāms of transmission knew him.'" In *Ghāyat al-bayān sharḥ al-Hidāyah*, "They transmit the ascription of weakness to him from Abū Ḥanīfah, but that ascription of weakness is not correct according to the books of ḥadīth. Whoever claims that is duty bound to explain himself." In *al-Bināyah* by al-ᶜAynī at the mention of the author of *al-Hidāyah* that Zayd ibn ᶜAyyāsh is weak according to the transmitters there is, "This is not correct. On the contrary he is a trustworthy narrator according to ḥadīth transmitters." In *at-Talkhīṣ al-ḥabīr*, "A group, among whom are aṭ-Ṭaḥāwī, aṭ-Ṭabarī, Ibn Ḥazm and ᶜAbd al-Haqq, regard this ḥadīth as defective because of the unknown character of Zayd, but the answer is that ad-Dāraquṭnī said, 'He is a firmly established trustworthy narrator,' and al-Mundhir said, 'Two trustworthy narrators transmitted from him and Mālik relied upon him along with the fact that he took extraordinary precautions [about his narrators]. At-Tirmidhī and al-Ḥākim declared it to be ṣaḥīḥ, and he said, "I do not know anyone who cast aspersions on him."'" In general the accusation that he is unknown has been completely removed from Zayd, both the fact that he himself is unknown or that his character is unknown, both of them by specific statements by the critical scholars of ḥadīth.

Zayd ibn Aslam Abū Usāmah, but some say Abū ᶜAbdullāh, was Zayd ibn Aslam al-ᶜAdawī the Madīnan, the faqīh, who was the mawlā of

Madīnah. Aḥmad, Abū Zurʿah, Abū Ḥātim, Muḥammad ibn Saʿd, an-Nasāʾī and Ibn Kharāsh said that he was a trustworthy narrator. Yaʿqūb ibn Shaybah said, "He was a trustworthy narrator of the people of fiqh and knowledge, and he had knowledge of commentary [of the Qurʾān]." He died in 136 AH, but some people say something else. Thus it is in *Tahdhīb at-tahdhīb* and it is similar in *Isʿāf al-mubaṭṭaʾ* of as-Suyūṭī.

Zayd ibn Khālid al-Juhanī is Abū ʿAbd ar-Raḥmān the Madīnan, but some say Abū Ṭalḥah or Abū Zurʿah. He was the man responsible for the banner of Juhaynah on the day or the Opening [of Makkah to Islam]. He died in 78 AH in Madīnah, but some say 68 AH and others say 50 AH, in Egypt, but some say in Kūfa at the end of the khilāfah of Muʿāwiyah, as is in *Isʿāf al-mubaṭṭaʾ* of as-Suyūṭī.

Zayd ibn Ṭalḥah was a minor Follower. Al-Ḥākim thought that he was a Companion, but it is not like that, as al-Ḥāfiẓ expanded upon in *al-Iṣābah*.

Zayd ibn Thābit. His honorific was Abū Saʿīd, but some say Abū Khārijah. He was an-Najjārī and Madīnan. He was the scribe of the revelation and one of those who collected all of the Qurʾān during the lifetime of the Messenger of Allah ﷺ. He died in 45 AH, but some say in 48 AH and others 51 AH, as is in *al-Isʿāf.* He was one of those "firmly rooted in knowledge" [see Qurʾān, Sūrah Āl ʿImrān: 7].

Zaynab was the eldest of the daughters of the Messenger of Allah ﷺ. She accepted Islam and emigrated when her husband refused to accept Islam. She died in the lifetime of the Messenger of Allah ﷺ in 8 AH, as is in *al-Istīʿāb*.

Zaynab bint Abī Salamah is the step-daughter of the Prophet ﷺ. Her mother was Umm Salamah, the mother of the believers, and her father was Abū Salamah ʿAbdullāh ibn Asad al-Makhzūmī the Companion, as is in *al-Istīʿāb* and elsewhere.

Zaynab bint Kaᶜb ibn ᶜUjrah was the wife of Abū Saᶜīd al-Khudrī. Ibn Ḥibbān regarded her as a trustworthy narrator, as as-Suyūṭī said in *al-Isᶜāf*.

Az-Zuhrī. See Ibn Shihāb az-Zuhrī.

Zurārah – as he spelt it in *al-Mughnī* – Ibn Abī Awfā, and it is thus in some copies. However, in many of the edited copies it is Ibn Awfā. He mentioned in *at-Tahdhīb* and elsewhere that he was Zurārah ibn Awfā al-ᶜĀmirī Abū Ḥājib the Baṣran. An-Nasā'ī, al-ᶜIjlī, Ibn Ḥibbān and others declared him a trustworthy narrator. He died in 93 AH according to what Ibn Saᶜd said, but others have said otherwise.

Bibliography

Dutton, Yasin, *The Origins of Islamic Law: The Qurʾān, the Muwaṭṭaʾ, and Madīnan ʿAmal,* Curzon Press, Surrey, 1999.

Ibn al-ʿArabī, Qāḍī Abū Bakr, *Defence Against Disaster* (translation of *al-ʿAwāṣim min al-qawāṣim*), Madinah Press, Cape Town, South Africa. 1995.

Ibn al-Athīr, Imām Majd ad-Dīn, *an-Nihāyah fi gharīb al-ḥadīth wa'l-athar,* Cairo 1965. Text from http://www.muhaddith.org.

Ibn Saʿd, *aṭ-Ṭabaqāt al-kubrā,* partially translated and published in English as *The Men of Madinah Vols. I & II,* and *The Women of Madinah,* by Aisha Bewley, Ta-Ha Publishing Ltd., London. 1995.

al-Laknawī, ʿAbd al-Ḥayy, *at-Taʿlīq al-Mumajjad li Muwaṭṭaʾ al-Imām Muḥammad* edited by Dr. Taqī ad-Dīn an-Nadwī, Dār al-Qalam, Damascus, first edition 1413 AH/1991 CE. Use was also made of the text from http://www.muhaddith.org.

Lane, E.W., *Arabic-English Lexicon,* The Islamic Texts Society, Cambridge, England, 1984.

Mālik ibn Anas, Imām, *al-Muwaṭṭaʾ* in the narration of Yaḥyā ibn Yaḥyā al-Laythī. Translated by Aisha Bewley and Yacoub Johnson. Madinah Press, Norwich, 1982.

al-Mālikī al-Ḥasanī, Muḥammad ibn ʿAlawī, *Anwār al-masālik ilā riwāyāt Muwaṭṭaʾ Mālik.* Doha, Qatar. Muḥarram 1400 AH.

as-Suyūṭī, Jalāl ad-Dīn, *Isʿāf al-Mubaṭṭaʾ bi rijāl al-Muwaṭṭaʾ*, Dār Iḥyāʾ al-Kutub al-ʿArabiyyah, Egypt.

A Madinan View

on the sunnah, courtesy, wisdom, battles and history

by

Abu Muhammad 'Abdullah
Ibn Abi Zayd al-Qayrawani
(d. 386 AH)

translated by

Abdassamad Clarke

Ta-Ha Publishers Ltd.
1 Wynne Road, London
SW9 0BB.

www.taha.co.uk